Going From
An Angry Man
To A Peaceful Man
Is Not An Easy Journey

by

James E. McCullough

DORRANCE
PUBLISHING CO
EST. 1920
PITTSBURGH, PENNSYLVANIA 15238

Dorrance Publishing Co
585 Alpha Drive
Pittsburgh, PA 15238
Visit our website at *www.dorrancebookstore.com*

ISBN: 978-1-6470-2533-5
eISBN: 978-1-6470-2703-2

The title of this book

Going From An Angry Man To A Peaceful Man Is Not An Easy Journey

Let me just start off by telling you that I can't tell you how to become rich or what it takes to get to that point.

I can't even tell you how to find Jesus because what I had to realize is that only through you can he be allowed to enter into your life.

Do something now in order for you to find him for yourself.

I can tell you what it's like to want to be comfortable and not have to struggle.

How when you see good things happening to other people and still trust God not always asking if you did something wrong all of the time when it appears no change is taking place in your life.

Your environment is not where you live, but what's inside of you and what you allow to come out.

We seek to find blame, but refuse to accept fault.

When or what occurred in your life that made you become angry at the world or God?

When did the peace leave your spirit and the hate replace it?

Not saying these questions will not come up in your life.

In the Bible in Luke 24:10, it talks about the day that Mary Magdalene, Joanna, Mary the mother of James, and the others with them who told this to the apostles.

How they went to the tomb not expecting to find that the stone in closing the body of Jesus to be rolled away and then to walk in and find that his body was not there.

As they started wondering how this could have happened, suddenly two men in clothes that gleamed like lighting stood beside them and as the women bowed down before them; they were asked this question, "Why are you looking for the living among the dead?"

Now they went back and told the apostles about what had taken place.

The only thing is that even though the apostles were told about what had taken place they did not believe they thought it was nonsense.

Peter got up and ran to the tomb to see for his self and found that what was told to him was true, he still could not take hold of what had taken place.

This is what we deal with every day of our lives and even though Jesus reveals to us what he has planned on blessing each one of us with, it's hard to believe that he keeps his word.

You see these people had been chosen by Jesus and walked and talked with him.

Yet through all that they had seen and been told and taught by Jesus they did not believe what was told to them by him.

You see this is not just them, but you and me as well. The finger points at me when I look in the mirror when I'm not always trusting in God.

Who does it point to when you look in the mirror?

Do you believe that Jesus can resurrect your life?

That's what this book in away deals with the resurrection from one way of life to another.

Going from anger to peace and from peace to love from love to God's will.

Chapter 1
Finding Out Who I am

Like most of you, I had no idea of God or Jesus.

The power between the two names and how they were one.

I heard a lot of different things, but I never really understood.

So, without me knowing, I began my journey of seeking the answer to the question, "Who is God and Jesus as well as the Holy Spirit?"

A lot of people pretend to know and they were following false prophets who would lead them to Hell instead of the embrace of the Father and the Son and that of the Holy Spirit.

I know this is real because if not for the love that Jesus had for me time and time again, I would have been led to death.

Real death with no chance of life.

Let me tell you about my journey in life or going from an angry man to a peaceful started.

My name is James McCullough I was born in Pittsburgh, Pa. Most of my childhood was pretty rough growing up.

God tends to take us on a journey no one really knows when our journey begins or when it ends.

God takes us on one journey, but there is a journey we must go on in order to find what we feel is needed or who is needed in our lives.

All of us are not looking to find the things of God of Heaven, but the things of the God of the earth or the worldly God.

You should be able to have answers to any questions along the way.

Part of that journey is wanting to belong, to fit in somewhere.

Question?

Fit in where and with whom?

Now in Psalms 3:8, it reads, "From the Lord comes deliverance. May your blessings be on your people." NIV

In Psalms 94:1 it reads, "O Lord. the God to whom vengeance belongs. O Lord of vengeance, let your glorious justice be seen." NLT

In Daniel 9:9, it reads "To the Lord our God belongs compassion and forgiveness, for we have rebelled against Him: nor have we obeyed the voice of the Lord our God, to walk in His teachings which He set before us through His servants the Prophets." NASB

In 1 Corinthians 7:32-3, it reads "But I would have you without carefulness. He that is unmarried careth for the things that belong to the Lord, how he may please the Lord? but he that is married careth for the things that are of the world, how to please his wife." KJV

It seems as though there are so many other groups and organizations that we want to belong because there are no laws or rules to be followed you just do as you feel and create your own freedom.

But what we need to realize is nothing is free you will pay a price one way or another.

Before I begin let me just say I have a wonderful family, but like most we all grow apart it's one of life's things that takes place.

When I was growing up, I wanted to belong and as I got older it became harder and harder to fit in with people because trust became a big issue for me it was harder because I was wanting to belong.

Have you ever been the black sheep of the family not really feeling like you belonged?

Can you pull up those memories without having feelings of anger?

Can you pull up those memories without feeling pain?

When you visit your family on holidays do you feel as though you fit in?

Do you know them other than they're your family by blood, but you still feel like a stranger?

If you answered yes to any of these questions some people may say you have a problem, but you don't.

There are so many people who feel like outcasts between family, friends, and even while in the church that they belong to.

That's why people turn to drugs, sex, and other vices along with suicide, just to name a few.

Wanting to belong is so important in society as a whole.

It always has been and it always will be.

But some people don't see this as being a problem or they may think that one is more important than the other.

But the choice you make one can lead to life.

But you have to realize the choices are not all the same.

The wrong one can lead to the life called death.

But again, don't get me wrong I still love my family, but I later in life had to realize that no matter how hard I wanted to belong or fit in, that person from my past had to learn to move on.

I had to learn to be happy with myself and that was not an easy walk.

Yes, I did stumble along the way no one is perfect.

That's why I am here writing this today to help you along the way and to help you on your journey.

So, if you're searching for something or someone that was missing in your life.

There are so many different things people use as a vice that brings in negative actions.

Please stop search for something you will never find.

If you lived life without this thing you seek for this long, what are you really missing?

Do you know anyone who just after waking up says to themselves "I think I'll sell my soul to the devil today? Because I don't like the way my life is at this point."

For some they don't realize they do this every waking day of their lives.

You may ask, "How could that be?"

The answer to the question is within your spirit.

For some people the gift's and promises of the world.

It seems to be far more rewarding then that which Jesus has promised.

That's just who they have become and until the change within them takes place before it's too late they will continue to live a life of giving themselves to Satan.

So many people believe that your time to choose right from wrong never runs out.

I am here to tell you how Jesus had to take me through what I had to go through in order for me to realize the path/journey I was headed towards.

Have you ever been hurt?

Have you ever gone through pain?

Have you ever had to deal with racism?

What is racism?

I looked this word up and it said that racism takes many forms and can happen in many places.

It includes prejudice, discrimination, or hatred directed at someone because of their color, ethnicity, or national origin.

But now get this, they also say that people often associate racism with acts of abuse or harassment.

However, it doesn't need to involve violent or intimidating behavior.

Take racial name-calling and jokes or consider situations when people may be excluded from groups or activities because of where they come from or because of who they are.

Racism is something that is revealed through the actions of others along with their attitudes.

Racism is more than just words, it is action.

When you can't forgive someone because of something they did to you at some point in your life, you are walking around as a racist.

Have you had someone tell you or have you ever told someone, "I will get you before you get me?"

That's a form of racism.

People change and we all move in different directions, even when it comes to family. I will always love mine, but the true people who held everyone together moved on a long time ago and now they await the return of Jesus.

The glue or the blood which ties us together is more like water and doesn't hold anything together anymore.

In our families these days it's like belonging to a gang if you don't fit in, you don't belong.

Along the way of becoming mature, what happened to the friends along the way?

You know those people that were in your life when all was going well for you, they seem to always be calling to check on you wanting to hang around you.

But for some reason life isn't looking so great for you because now you're starting to lose things and it seems as though that with which you had is gone.

Wow!

My question is, where are all of the so-called friends and family?

What happened to the phone calls and the gatherings and hang outs?

That which was not true will not stand.

For most that causes anger to show its face for some depression, lack of trust of others, disappointment, hurt, and pain.

Which now leads you to become a racist.

Just imagine if Jesus had the same attitude.

This is something to think about for both believers and non-believers.

Jesus is real and he did die for us all.

The Bible says that God the Heavenly Father wanted to destroy us all because of the way that we are now.

There are so many people with no spirit no soul.

Who are you?

What category do you fall into?

I walked around not knowing the answer to the questions.

The thing is, I thought I knew it all.

You see, growing up the way I did I didn't realize how I was hurting others because I thought it was normal.

How many of you are not seeing this in yourself?

A lot of times we may act this way around a group of friends.

If you had the chance to be in a group with friends, people that you think would be there for you.

Who would you choose?

Let's say one friend.

With most of us, our first choice would not be Jesus.

Truth be told.

In the beginning or the start of our life if someone was to ask you, "Whose side do you want to belong or be on?" You should first ask, "What do you mean?"

No one gives you an explanation as to what they are talking about.

So, you start looking around to see the different choices your able to pick from still not sure.

Because most people are moving away from God because they are not able to please their flesh and their eyes.

People's bodies are not looked upon as being holy temples.

They look at the body as something to be taken and destroyed.

In other words, something to conquer.

But while this is taking place, the mind is being slowly taken and stripped of one's identity and then one's spirit.

I remember when I wanted to belong so badly because I just didn't feel accepted during my childhood by my family or friends.

You see because I felt this way I didn't know where I belonged or who I was either.

I just didn't feel accepted by anyone.

But there where those few who God placed in my life that as I went through my struggles and the pain that burned in my soul.

They were there to help take my mind off of the things going on in my spirit in order for me to put a smile on my face.

The thing is I was one of those who just wanted to take and destroy, but I used to think that there were those that the Lord would allow me to harm.

Do you believe this to be true?

GOING FROM AN ANGRY MAN TO A PEACEFUL MAN
IS NOT AN EASY JOURNEY

I want you to look within yourself and find the answer because there is a certain way of life we all live and a different truth we all live.

The thing is are you willing to allow God to enter into your life and have his will?

Who do you pray too and who do you call father?

Without knowing it, Jesus had starting me on my journey.

This is a question I want to ask you for those of you who know Jesus.

Have you ever felt alone after giving your life to Him?

Now I want to ask you who don't know Jesus, as well as those who refuse to acknowledge him.

Do you feel alone in the world?

Has hurt and pain and unforgiveness taken away trust in wanting to belong?

For those of you who now follow Jesus before then, did you feel like you were living in a world of darkness searching for some type of light to guide you?

When you were in the world were you one of the so-called cool guys or girls.

The life of the party while you were around all your friends or just out drinking, smoking, or whatever you were doing that made you feel like the life of the party.

But when you got home you felt so alone.

When you decided that you would allow God to rule your life the Heavenly Father, did things change in a way that you didn't understand?

Were there people who wanted to destroy your character by telling lies on you and then turn around and lie to you?

Did the devil begin to use the good in you through someone else to try and make you feel like you had become this person not worthy to be called a child of God?

Did they try to say that you are not a man or woman?

How did it make you feel?

The real thing that Satan wants to do is to kill, steal, and destroy your relationship with Jesus.

How does he do that?

By destroying the relationship with yourself.

Did you know that at that point to forget who you were and not see who you have become?

For a lot of people having wealth can make them angry and sometimes lost.

What was it that you gained that made you walk away from Jesus?

What would make you sell your soul?

Who would make you sell your soul?

These are real questions because it's happening more and more in this time that we are living and will increase as time goes on.

Why would you want to lose what you could have with Jesus?

There are those who have lost their way… lost their minds.

I see this so much with the leaders of the church as well.

Wealth is supposed to be used to expand the kingdom near and far.

But the attitude towards helping near has become lost so greatly that most of the time people have stopped seeing and put blinders on.

Do you have to be a drug dealer in order to give back to the people?

They give back but they also keep them captive with the drugs.

This is what Satan does also he gives but he holds you captive with what he gives you.

They give in order to take it back by suppling the drugs.

But the thing is most of them give from the heart because they not only help the drug users but those they see have a need.

People of God the Heavenly Father, wants to know what really happened to the relationships in the different communities?

Times are changing are we not worried.

I used to be so mad and angry at my father for the way he treated me growing up.

And as I got older, I learned to hate him more and more.

For the longest time, I could only see the abuse both mental and physical.

The beatings the punishments being accused and made to feel like I wanted to die.

But I began to lose myself and that's when the darkness took over my body, I felt dead inside.

I began not care about no one but me.

All of the feelings for anyone else were gone.

I became lost it became hard being alone.

I had to learn how to become the life of the party.

I received all kinds of favor, but it came with a price at that time not for me but for those who were around me, or so I thought.

Life was good and the money I made was great.

But it didn't start out like that. I was, in other words, made to feel like a step-child most of my life.

Roaming not always knowing where I would lay my head.

Whose house was I going to be at?

You see my mother made some bad choices after my father as well as with the men in her life.

When your young you may go through things and not know or understand.

The big question.

Why me?

You see, I did not know my father was abusive to my mother, I just knew he was that way to me.

To make matters worse, the men she was dealing with wanted her to put me out and then come to find out they were abusive to her as well.

You see, my mother was raising me, my sister, and my little brother.

I remember a lot of fun times, trips, and doing these things as a family.

But I had no idea how bad my mom was struggling to feed us and clothe us and keep a roof over or heads.

I know there are a lot of single parents that are out there that are struggling.

Hold on, help is on the way.

But you see now days most women want them bad boys and most men want them bad girls.

So, most of the time things don' t work out.

· Also, nowadays it's about what you have, not who you are inside.

Money and objects have become more to people their God.

It's so alive in the church today in ways that I know are not pleasing to God.

Can I share something with you?

I remember one fun time with my father he had this red convertible and he picked me and my sister up and took us out for ice cream and candy.

Can you remember any nice thing throughout your life that allows you to forgive someone?

I had no idea that I had become my father in the way that had made me hardened my heart.

When my father died, that's when I found out how much we had in common.

I wish we had become friends in life instead of not wanting to deal with each other, know my dad could cook and bake.

I would have love to had been able to spend time with him teaching me some of his secrets on cooking.

I wish I could have had a father I could have looked up to in order for me to fill that void of disappointment knowing I had a father I never knew until the day he died.

I know there are a lot of people who feel the same way with either their mother or father.

But we have to let go of the ghost and stop chasing the past live for now or else it will ripe your whole life apart.

The pain you went through is there to build your faith and make you stronger.

Now know that you are loved even when you don't feel it or even when you feel you don't have people in your life.

The Heavenly Father and Jesus are there with you at all times. So when you're feeling down, call on that great name, the name like no other, Jesus.

It may hurt and it may to you seem like there is no one there for you.

Please think again. Please don't give up.

I have struggled so much in my life, but I am still here.

It's not easy.

Now let me please take you back to wealth.

You forget how hard and how much work and faith along with prayer it took to become financially blessed.

When you start believing that you did this on your own you are forgetting that it was received through God.

It's like you have the wealth but you have not discovered things have changed.

But to you, nothing has changed but the people you hang out with.

You walk around angry at the world, but more so at yourself because you are still you and the people of the world are still the same people that intend to use you for what they can get.

To lose what you have and have to start all over again can sometimes bring peace because you know what it's like to have and now you know what's it's like to have not.

For most it does not make you but allows you to make it.

For some people when they lose something, they feel that they have lost it all.

So, they don't feel life is worth living so they take their own life at their own hand.

How many of you, if you had to start over, would learn to live your life with less stress and learn how to have more fun rediscovering yourself?

Trust me, I'm not saying it's easy getting to that point because it's not.

I did a lot of crying out to Jesus asking why me?

I had no idea of the pain I would face dealing with the disappointment from man.

But God will teach you how to have faith in Him by allowing you to learn how to trust in Him.

Peace is not found in things nor is it found in the people you place around you; but in God and Jesus.

Chapter 2
If I take you, I win

When I first sat down to write this book, I had no idea what sacrifice was like nor what it takes to make a sacrifice.

I was always use to living my life and only looking out for myself.

One who was only living for what they could get from someone or what they can get out of someone.

That person misses out on the sacrifice another makes for them in prayer.

Most of the time it's not by choice, even when you pray and fast and begin to ask God what did I do and what am I doing wrong.

Most people acknowledge Jesus and seem to know his name, but not what it stands for nor what it means to call on his name.

Because they want what does not belong to them or what they are not supposed to have.

I had to learn the hard way the difference between a sacrifice of the heart and a sacrifice of a selfish individual who is only thinking of themselves.

When Jesus was crucified it was because people didn't believe who he was or respect what he did, even though he was the gift that was given to them.

He was also the gift whose life was given because of their ignorance.

They could not understand Jesus so they became afraid of him because he took the attention away from them.

With him around no one else could be heard or seen.

Yet these are the so-called people of God.

God gave, but he knows that man could not handle what was given to them.

Yet still God gave of Himself, Jesus the gift of life.

People from that time had to deal with that mistake all the rest of their days. Even now, people have the mind set of that era and even though they found out who Jesus truly was.

They still reject him even now.

I, too, have had to live with a mistake from my teen years.

Not believing in myself or the love I had for one woman and a child.

When I walked away, I didn't realize that I sacrificed love.

Instead of learning about love, I learned how to be a selfish man of no respect.

Has God ever given you a job to do and instead of completing the job, you tried to run from it, not realizing that it would come back around to you again?

Have you ever done something and said it was for the glory of God and tried to use it for your own gain instead?

Did it make you feel bad?

Did you repent?

I hope your answer to both questions were, "yes."

I guess for those of you who don't understand the questions.

I wrote a book called *Understanding the Power of God.*

Most people think that because you chose this life of following Jesus, all of a sudden it makes you become a nerd.

Most even believe that it makes you better then someone else, a lot of people get it twisted.

You're still the same person, only now you have a different goal set in your life.

The higher power you are now seeking is asking you to change from your sinful and selfish ways to a walk of righteousness.

But no matter who you are, you will never get this walk in life right all of the time.

This is because you have just become Jesus's chosen for this time right now.

Not to be greater in away but less.

He has always had his eye on you, but He knew at the time you were not ready to receive Him.

Sometimes we have to go through some things, but the trails and lessons of life it only makes us stronger.

But again, it's not easy.

Jesus already knows what people that will make it so to full fill the calling. He knows if you can't handle the small tests.

How can you get through the real life situations?

When Jesus sets our path in life to do the work and the will of the Father it's not easy at all so he needs to make you ready.

Growing up for me as a teenager was different only because no matter what I was going through I would just pick myself up and move on.

This was because I did not feel as though I belonged anywhere.

Growing up I felt like I was adopted my father did not want me and neither did my mother.

I wanted so much to belong.

So, from fear of not belonging and fear of giving love but not getting it back I had a hardened heart, but did not realize it because I did not know Jesus or the word of God.

In Psalms 51:5 KJ, "Behold, I was shapen in iniquity: and in sin did my mother conceive me."

So, by me being this way I had the opportunity to live in other states and I never found myself being afraid of change.

Do you know when you truly accepted Jesus into your life he reveals your fears?

If you really want to know what you are afraid of, look into a mirror.

Do you know when he called you into His life for you become His?

Once Jesus takes a hold on you, don't let go, don't cut the lifeline because it's your life he's trying to save and Jesus is the energy source you need.

Not only in this life but into the next.

When everything in your life seemed to be going great and yet you still were unhappy.

This was the reason Jesus called on you because he knew that you felt like life was just not worth living anymore.

People, we need to stop pretending that we're happy and we really are trying to make people think that we have this beautiful life.

But we cry at night and we get to the point of feeling alone and afraid of being alone.

We all have a different story.

Do you mind if I share mine with you?

I would like to share with you when I believe I truly accepted Jesus into my life.

This was also the time in which I was actually able to hear the voice of the Lord.

Even though I thought I knew God because I had been searching to seek his face and his will in my life, I thought I had found Him.

Only to realized I had not found the Lord, only myself, my will, and I saw how I still continued to live my life my way.

But you see, all my life I lived a lie because I thought that I was the man.

I felt and believed that I didn't need anyone in my life.

I just knew that I had it all and knew it all as well.

I even began to believe that my walk with the Lord was on point.

Only to find out that I was so wrong even then.

It was not about me finding God, but God accepting me as one of his own.

You see, we are all chosen but how many are accepted?

So, for me to say that my true walk had actually begun sometime in the summer of the year 2008 may not be correct.

I want to say that's when God spoke to me and gave me the words to write in a book.

This was the first time I had ever written a book or anything like that.

The book I am talking about is called *Understanding the Power of God: Is your Marriage Pleasing to God or Just Yourself?*

You see, I didn't understand what God had me write and I didn't realize he was asking me the questions in the book.

I tried to rush everything in order to put the book out and Satan grab hold of it and things did not work the way I thought it would.

But I need you to understand that he was also speaking the truth about things going on in my life.

I was always trying to rush things or people were trying to rush me.

One of the biggest questions He asked, but I didn't Know what the answer was.

That question was, "Is my marriage pleasing to Him or just myself?"

To put it another way, was God getting the glory in my marriage or was the devil getting the glory through my actions?

Whose life was I living and whose will was I serving?

We also need to ask if the way the way we are living our life is it right?

Is it pleasing with the Heavenly Father or only right with one self?

I had no idea at the time how to answer that question either.

God had to show me in another way just where I stood.

I also have to tell you when God shows you something it does not always feel good to you, but how do you think it makes Jesus feel?

After starting the first book I felt that the move to Atlanta was a mistake, because I began to lose everything I had.

But how can you blame you're actions on a place or another person.

I couldn't figure out why this was happening to me and why I couldn't make it stop.

I continued to pray to God asking him, "What I am doing wrong?"

Everything was being taken away from me and I didn't understand.

My wife walked out on me again and took the cat with her. I was losing everything.

I began to question myself about the way I was loving her and if I was loving her the right way.

You have to understand I never truly knew how to love someone.

God allowed me to be able to keep my two dogs Phoenix and Dotson.

Sometimes it's not always the people that will remain.

Jesus then said to me, "The dogs will always chose the one who loves them, but you as humans will only chose that which pleases the flesh."

That's why it's so rare to find people that are truly in a relationship with each other through Jesus.

So, God allowed me to keep the two things that would teach me how to love as well as the meaning of sacrifice, my two dogs Nix and Dot.

Let me ask you this question: How does it feel when the one you loved walks out on you?

Do you become blinded by the lack of faith that Jesus will heal your heart and spirit once more?

For some they will fall from the grace of God with no way to return.

What happens when doubt takes over?

The question is in your time of doubt whose name are you going to call?

Did you know that in life there is a chain of command?

There is a chain of command in Heaven.

The Heavenly Father, Jesus, and the Holy Spirit.

The Holy Spirit leads, guides, comforts, and so much more.

Jesus saves and listens to all of your complaints and calls you back when you stray and he seeks the lost.

Jesus also goes before the Father in your name when you call his and seeks the will and forgiveness of the Father in your behalf, again so much more.

Yet we still have an unbelief of God's word and his promise for us that he will restore that which was lost in his name.

Before I begin my journey, I just wanted to let you know how hate had taken over my heart.

But it was only the beginning of me learning to understand the power of God, only I didn't know it at the time.

Did you know that it takes more energy to hate then to love?

That's why a lot of people who walk around with so much hatred in their spirits get sick and have a lot of problems.

Try smiling and saying, "Hello" more and see the change that comes over your life.

I was at the lowest point in my life or so I thought.

I was losing everything and now I was about to be put out on the street. I didn't know what to do.

I continued asking God what I should do.

18

Jesus then spoke to me and said that the truth will always free the soul.

He loves me even when I do wrong or even when I reject Him.

He then began to teach me that when you can still love someone when you feel your heart and soul had been taken from your body.

He then said to me, "James, that's when you can understand how much I love you."

Not that God has to deal with the things that we do, but he said that there are times your actions are so hurtful to me.

But because I love you, I forgive you and bless you because you are my child.

You see even in your greatest time of pain and hurt when you say and do things that could affect your eternal life.

Jesus knows what you are feeling and specks on your behalf for forgiveness.

Yes, just like you I asked the Lord, "If you love me how could you allow me to go through so much pain?"

He then said calmly, "Sometimes when you see the wind blow and you stand and listen with your ear's shut, you can hear me say a change is about to take place in your life. As you begin to open your ears and your eye's you can see a change in seasons, but not seasons as man say's seasons change, but as seasons that change in the spirit."

In the book of Ecclesiastes: 9:1 & 2 It says, "So I reflected on all this and concluded that the righteous and the wise and what they do are in God's hands, but no man knows whether love or hate awaits him."

All share a common destiny the righteous and the wicked, the good and the bad, the clean and the unclean, those who offer sacrifices and those who do not.

As it is with the good man, so with the sinner; as it is with those who takes oaths, so with those who are afraid to take them.

That's what made me seek God even more because I said to Jesus no matter how one would treat me never let my heart harden against anyone in need of a hand from me.

But Lord, you must teach me once more how to have a gentle hands.

I've tried helping people who were or said that they were about to become homeless.

I wasn't really looking for anything from them, I just wanted to help because of the way I felt after the final rejection and how God delivered me.

I would like to say a prayer

Heavenly Father Lord God Almighty, I come before you, your humble servant, asking Lord God for forgiveness for the actions of those who have allowed their hearts to harden even myself. When it comes to helping someone and they are rejected by that same person they may have asked. I ask that the one who was on the end of being turned away would find it in their hearts to forgive.

We as flesh find it at times easier to try and get so called even because we feel we have the upper hand, even though we fell to realize that the upper hand has and will always be yours Lord God.

So, Father God as we go through the spiritual seasonal changes we deal with things in a way that does not challenge our faith or walk with you but reflects our trust in you and belief in your word and all that it says.

For Heavenly Father, if we are truly yours, no one can pluck us from your hands.

Father God in this I pray that we all may be saved in the mighty name of our Lord Jesus. Amen.

So, I began to say Heavenly Father I would never want for anyone to go through the pain that I had to deal with in this situation of having no one to turn too.

But because of who our God is, he made a way.

But you see that was only because I did not realize that all of my life, Lord Jesus, you were there for me.

God showed me how to begin to live my life all over again in a way that I never knew I could live only I did not realize it until later in life.

I started to realize that even though it seemed my world was falling apart I had to give God the glory.

This took a lot of time and praying and crying before the Lord day and night.

The pain was greater than me, but not greater than God.

I had to replay everything I did over and over again until I began to forgive myself.

It was not done to hurt me but to strengthen me. Otherwise, it would have destroyed me.

God showed me the difference between love and hate.

He first had to show me how to stop hating myself for the mistakes that I had made in life.

That was the only way he could teach me how to love.

Did you know that when you learn to love you learn to feel?

Will you take a look at yourself from the inside out and ask Jesus what's in your heart?

This is only because in order for this to take place, you have to let him heal the hurt as well as the pain.

Jesus also reminded me of some of the things he taught me through the writing of book one.

Jesus showed me that sometimes he will take something away in order for us to be able to reach our purpose.

It has been a very lonely and painful experience during this walk into God's will and purpose for my life.

I had to be taken away from everyone and placed in a state of isolation away from the world in order to hear what God had to tell me.

I needed to find a quiet place, I even needed to get away from the noise within my own spirit.

Jesus asked me, "Are you willing to go through whatever it takes in order to truly understand the will and purpose that my Father has for your life. Can you trust in me and my Father to lead you through this journey and believe that no harmed or death will come to you?"

My answer was, "Yes."

Your first step is the Bible.

But like everyone else, I get a little weary at times and have to keep praying to God to keep me strong and keep me focused on the truth and the hope of the truth.

We seem to always lose hope because we don't believe in the truth.

Jesus began to show me something I did in my teens that has always troubled my heart and spirit and for the longest I would not talk about it to anyone.

Whenever my spirit would become troubled, God would take me to a mountain top and there, he would remind me that someone was missing in my life.

The only thing about it was that I did not want to face that part of my life because I was ashamed of what I had did.

I would always think to myself how could someone forgive me for what I did.

This time he took me to the mountains, it was the Blue Ridge Mountains in Georgia. My heart and spirit were opened to receive what was needed to start book number two.

But most of all to heal me from all of the pain that I was dealing with in my heart.

When I sat down and begin to think about the questions that were asked of me, it all added to one major question, which was.

"What are you willing to sacrifice?"

Have you ever had someone ask you, "What do you think you would be doing in five years?"

In thinking about the answer to that question, one should ask themselves, "Do I know who I am know?"

Because if you're not sure of who you are, how can you say were you will be?

Jesus began to deal with me about my chances of being able to have an opportunity to get into the kingdom of Heaven, as well as all of the things I would have to go through in order for this to happen.

The key words are all of the things, not some.

I had no idea what was laying ahead of me, but he said, "You must first learn who you are before you can decide to whom you belong."

So, the first thing was allowing me to stand on water in a way of speaking, not on shaky ground.

This was so that he could place my feet on a rock, a firm foundation in order for me to learn how to be a son, not a stranger.

If you don't know Jesus is the solid rock; find out for yourself who he is as I am still doing every day of my life.

A leader, yet a servant.

The life that I've had to live for the past few years has been hard.

Through the grace of our Lord and Savior Christ Jesus, I was able to make it through a journey from Hell and back.

The only thing, it's not over yet, but even through it all Jesus took those emotions of disappoint and turned them into hope.

Now, not to say I don't still deal with the emotions of disappoint, because I do, but this time in myself.

He began to take the feeling of hurt and pain and turned it into love.

Jesus knew that in order for me to go through every challenge that has been chosen for me to go through, I needed to learn to trust in the Lord and not give up hope.

I had to realize that even though I couldn't see away out he was there to see me through.

The thing to also realize is that even when it's past the last minute that something was to take place, trust in him anyway and walk through it.

Don't forget that he has been bringing you out all this time and has not let you down. He's just building your faith and making you stronger.

Get ready because this is where the new journey begins and the old way of life ends.

But before I begin, let me ask you this question, "Are you willing to change to improve yourself for self-gain or are you willing to change in order to gain God's will in your life?"

The change I speak of will last forever, not until you get what you want or you get tired of what you have.

So, I need you to think about your answer because it will come up again.

I know at one point or another you have heard someone say, "Be careful how you treat someone because it will come back to you a hundred-fold."

The thing is, you never know when you are entertaining an angel.

In Hebrews 13:2, do not forget to entertain strangers, for by so doing some people have entertained angels without knowing it.

Now this is in the Bible. It's not my word, but God's word.

So that makes me think if we are to entertain strangers because they may be angels, what about the people that God places in our lives?

People like our husbands or our wives. What about our children? It could be anyone.

I also need you to understand that there are angels we are not to entertain.

The book of Revelation 12:7 through 12, "...And there was a war in Heaven. Michael and his angels fought against the dragon, and the dragon and his angels fought back. But he was not strong enough, and they lost their place in Heaven. The great dragon was hurled down-that ancient serpent called the devil, or Satan, who leads the whole world astray.

"He was hurled to the earth and his angels with him.

"Then I heard a loud voice in Heaven say:

"'Now have come the salvation and the power and the kingdom of our God, and the authority of his Christ.

"For the accuser of our brothers, who accuses them before our God day and night, has been hurled down.'

"They overcame him by the blood of the Lamb and by the word of their testimony; they did not love their lives so much as to shrink from death.

"Therefore rejoice, your Heavens and you who dwell in them!

"But woe to the earth and the sea, because the devil has gone down to you!

He is filled with fury, because he knows that his time is short".

This is something that people seem to forget, Satan will send his angels and say that they are from God in Heaven.

But through the power given by God himself, Satan is a God on earth and what seems to be taken place is that more and more people are entertaining Satan's angels and not God's.

But again, listen to what the Bible says, "his time is short". That's why he lies and he is given power to take those who freely give themselves to him and at this time his powers seem so strong.

But it's your desires that are strong and the satisfaction of your flesh has been awoken even more.

But know if you give yourself to Jesus, his power is the greatest because His power comes straight from the Father which is on high.

Let me put it this way who you follow will make a big difference and whatever is done to someone else will be done to you whether it be good or bad.

Let me start off with this word and the word is Karma; karma is the overall effect of one's behavior, held in Hinduism and Buddhism to determine one's destiny in a future existence.

Psalms 62: 11-12 one thing God has spoken two things I have heard; that you, O God, are strong, and that you, O Lord, are loving.

Surely you will reward each person according to what he has done.

You may not be rewarded for your deeds whether right or wrong in this life, but please understand it will happen in the next.

As far as I know, before we go into the next life we will have to stand before Jesus during judgment.

Only at this point there is nothing you can say because you'll be standing in front of Jesus pleading your case.

The sad part of that is some people will still be thinking the decision is theirs to make.

Not realizing that the decision was already made before they got there, it was already determined if they were heading to Heaven or Hell.

We will all be dealt with according to how we may have responded to others in our manors and behavior towards them during our life here on earth.

So, answer this question, "Who do you want to win your soul?"

Chapter 3

How can we walk away from a gift that which is God's love and not feel his disappointment?

We take a lot of things for granted and you know, sometimes it takes God to put us in a situation so that we are able to hear him speak to us because if you allow Jesus, he will give you a chance to make the wrongs you have done right.

God does this so that we may have the opportunity to make amines for our wrong doing in order to still have a chance to have a place in his kingdom.

So, I would like to share with you something that may have had an affect or may be the root cause to why I may have had to go through what I did in my marriage as well as my life.

Remember that word karma?

I don't know if what I am about to share with you, may have had a direct affect or may have played a part or may have been the reason as to why my ex-wife walked out on me and why the love stop within myself.

The only thing is I'll never know the answer to that question along with many others.

I would first like to repent and ask for forgiveness from a beautiful woman by the name of Sabina Johnson.

This is something I never shared with anyone, so please forgive me Sabina, you know what I am talking about.

First, let me say that this was the woman God gave me as a wife. She was the missing rib from my body and I could not see it at the time.

When I was growing up, I guess you could say that I was a troubled young man. Even then I didn't know who I was or who I was to become.

I was placed in a group home setting by chose in a way.

The group home was located in a remote area so if you were to even thinking about leaving, you would think twice.

Now when I think about what had taken place in my life during, or should I say after the decision, that I made after a phone call I received.

I being to think about a song that God placed in my spirit called, "Lord make me whole again".

But know I sing another song "Lord can you hear me". You see, I had no idea how bad I hurt you because I am still hurting.

I have never gotten over you or what I did.

Nothing I do or say can ever change what I did, so I ask you both to forgive me.

Now while at this facility, I had the chance of meeting the most beautiful girl in the world to me.

Her name?

Sabina!

I believe when our eyes met, we fell in love with each other.

Now Sabina was this beautiful mixed young woman but she appeared to look more white than black. She had the most beautiful brown frizzy hair. Her eyes and smile made my heart melt away.

I believe that her spirit even made God smile down on both of us.

I remember after the formal introduction to the facility I was led to the activity building.

I walked in and as they began to explain to me in more detail about the facility, I happened to look across the room.

I remember standing there listening to the counselors talking to some of the staff members and as I looked across the room that's when I noticed Sabina talking to some of her friends.

She was talking to them but looking over at me. I remember telling myself, "That girl over there, she's going to be my girlfriend. Watch!"

So, I walked over to her and asked her name.

She told me, "Sabina".

We talked for a while before it was time to head back to our dorms.

I could not wait until the next day to see her again.

After a while, things started going good between us and we began taking walks together and talking more.

So, I asked her if she would like to be my girl.

She said yes.

Have you ever seen or felt pure love?

That's what we had and at the time I had no idea what that was.

I had no idea that God had given me my first wife.

Now when I first met her, of course, I could not let her know how glad I was to have her say yes to our walk.

I need you to put in mind a picture.

The location of the facility was in a country setting that was in a mountain terrain, and it was day time and a beautiful day.

The face of the woman you are with, her beauty blends in with what God has created. Her smile as warm as the sun.

When she would laugh, it was as if the birds in the air were singing just to me.

Her voice like that of a calming rain fall that just put you in a relaxed state of mind.

It was as if it was only me and her alive on earth, no one else.

Now place in your mind a field of grass and trees that made a fence.

Now as you walk you took a path. At the end of the path, you came to this open area.

The sun was slowly beginning to set and the stars began to come out.

It was the most breath-taking sight you ever wanted to see.

The beautiful part of the beauty around me was Sabina.

While we were walking, the sun was setting and the moon and the stars were coming out.

As the moon began to shine, I looked over at Sabina and she had a glow about her like that of an angel.

As I glanced at her, I was thinking to myself, "If I could reach up and grab a star I would do so and I would place it on her finger and say, 'This is a gift from God. He has allowed me to give to you. I would have you if you would have me.'"

Sabina, you would be my wife. I did not know it at the time.

Instead, I held the gift God gave me in my arms and joy overtook me.

We walked and found a spot in the grass that was over near a row of trees in the open field.

So, we sat and talked and decided to lay down and we began to talk more and look deeper into each other's eyes.

Just looking at each other and not even realizing how the stars made the night that much more romantic and then we began to kiss and hold each other.

When people talk about something being perfect, that was it.

It just seemed as though we had been waiting for each other and we began to fall in love

You know some people are drawn together with sex and not love.

We walked around talking more each day and became boyfriend and girlfriend, enjoying life and each other.

Now after dating for a while and being with each other, we had two friends, Todd and Jeanie.

Todd's aunt was going out of town for a week so we decided to find a way to get to Todd's aunt's house while she was out of town.

We arranged for a ride so it was me, Sabina, Todd, and his girlfriend Jeanie.

We arrived at Todd's aunt's house where we stayed for five nights and six days.

GOING FROM AN ANGRY MAN TO A PEACEFUL MAN
IS NOT AN EASY JOURNEY

I remember it was the greatest time I ever had. The reason being that real love was in our hearts for each other.

One of the great moments I also remember was when we were sitting in the tub with each other talking and laughing, washing each other, not wanting our time together to end.

Wow!

The time together to never end.

Now after our little vacation was over, we decided to head back and face the music. We knew that we were in trouble, but we knew it wouldn't be for too long, or so we thought.

But the punishment seemed like forever because we were not able to see each other during the phase of our punishment.

I remember after we had been back for a while, I was showing off and jumped on the back of one of the activity buses.

A boy being a boy.

The driver did not know I was there and as he began to pick up speed, I jumped off.

Can you say stupid move?

Let's just say stupid.

I got all scraped up, but by the grace of God that's all that happened along with my pride being a little... well, you know.

About two to three months had passed from the time we had spent together and I was called to the nurse's office.

Now when I arrived, I noticed that Sabina was crying.

I didn't know what was going on, so the first thing that came to my mind was that we were in trouble and then the nurse laid it on me.

She said, "James do you know what happens when two people have sexual intercourse with each other? Do you know what it means when a woman starts to miss her menstrual cycle?"

At the time I didn't know.

She then told me that Sabina was pregnant.

When she told me that, I was so happy.

I was happy!

What no one knows is that she had become the love of my life and she has always been.

There has not been a day that has gone by that I have not thought about her, seeing her face, or wondering about our child.

Now a few months or so after I had received the good news, I got some bad news and that was they were moving me to another facility, but the funny thing was it was in her hometown.

Now Sabina was from McKeesport, PA. Out of all the places they could have sent me, it was to her hometown.

After that, contact was lost for some time between me and Sabina. But you know, God kept showing up in our lives.

But I did not know how to hear God's voice at that time.

All the signs were there to see.

Somehow Sabina found me and paid me a visit I really felt bad because she was pregnant and her belly was out there. It was during the winter season. Also, due to the fact that they moved me to another facility, she found me.

I guess they felt that this would be a way of splitting us apart in order for the both of us to lose interest in each other, so that we would forget about each other.

But that was not what Jesus had planned for us.

When Sabina found me, I was so happy to see her.

Of course, her stomach was bigger. I remember her beautiful little cheeks where red because she was cold and her nose was red too.

I was supposed to go to class that day, but I decided not to go and spend the day with her.

Seeing her that day was truly a blessing for me, but at the time I did not know what a blessing was.

I did not know who Jesus was at that time in my life.

I wish even to this day I had known Him.

So, we both went into the building; we had to sneak into the building in order to stay warm while we were together.

We had a wonderful time as we spent the day together talking until we both fell asleep holding each other.

Time went by and we decided that it was time for her to get ready to head home it was getting late and I wanted her to get home before school let out.

I really didn't want her to leave.

I never wanted to have her leave out of my life.

I was still head over heels in love with her and to this day I have never stopped.

What I didn't realize was that God had given me my own angel as well as a gift of love which was a child.

During this time in my life I didn't know Jesus, I didn't know myself.

After a while I returned back to my mother's house.

It was sometime after returning home a few weeks or so went by I received a phone call from Sabina and her little sister.

I tell you Sabina knew how to find me.

I have to share something with you about Sabina.

When I was with her, I was a proud black man who had love pumping through my body.

Walking with her seeing her smile holding her hand feeling her warm kiss and her warm embraces.

Looking in her eyes I could see my soul.

She was my hope.

Not a day has gone by that I have not asked myself, "Why?"

How could I have made such a bad mistake?

WOW!

I did.

Hmm.

The thing is Sabina and her little sister they were both so happy and they told me that I had a daughter.

We had a daughter.

I said, "Wow!"

It's a girl.

I have a little girl.

I was so happy and then out of nowhere fear set in, that's not the worst part.

As the fear set in, I began to think about how I would have to become responsible and my freedom would be over.

After receiving such wonderful news, I said the most hurtful thing any man could ever say to a woman.

Do you remember how I bragged about loving her?

I never stopped.

But I mentioned how much I loved her quite a few times, so what did I say to Sabina and our little sister.

First, I would like to repent for what I said to them both, because I told them not to ever call me again.

So, I am asking of you both for your forgiveness.

I have been living with that regret all my life the words I spoke on that day.

I remember maybe a year or so went by and I believe God was giving another chance to correct my mistake.

God allowed me to run into her again I had just finished helping my cousin move and went outside for a minute and who comes walking up the street, but Sabina.

I still see her even when I talk about this.

I wanted so much to hold her in my arms and say to her, "This time I'm not letting you get away."

But I could not get my body to do what my mind was thinking.

I wanted to tell her I was so sorry.

I wanted to run to her and say, "Sabina, how is our daughter?"

I wanted to take her in my arms and hold her and tell her that I loved her and to forgive me please.

I wanted to tell her how much I still loved her and I wanted us to get back together and raise our daughter.

But again, my pride got in the way.

I put my head down and I walked away never forgetting the look on her face.

The look of, "Why? What happened?"

I believe that's what I thought love was also.

My dad was not really a great part of my life and me and my mother were not really getting a long that well.

So what did I know about love?

What did I know about sacrificing one's self for love and family?

Sabina, I want you and our daughter to know there's nothing more than I would like to do then to change my words as well as my action, but I can't.

All I can say is I have seen what happens when we don't forgive and hold on to hate.

I see it every time I look in the mirror.

I did not hate Sabina I was hurt, but I can't imagine how much I hurt her.

There have been quite a few times I tried to find you.

I have been praying to God to let me find you.

I can't blame you if you don't want me in your lives.

I was wrong.

I can also tell you what pride can do to change your future and let you know what God can do to change your life.

Sabina I still see the stars in your eyes and smell your breath from the remembrance of our first kiss you are the love of my life I let get away without a fight and not fighting for.

It took a long time for me to learn to love again, but not only did I hurt you two I hurt someone else that became a part of my life her name is Terrie Dent you both would have liked her a lot and I know she would have liked you.

She has a new life and has since moved on and so have I.

So, through the mistakes and the disappointments I have made in life myself, I pray that God will heal all hearts and bring true forgiveness for all.

Now by no means is there any excuse for my reaction in the way I handled the situation, because I made a very bad choice.

I know that there are so many young men and women who at some point in their lives have done something that they regret doing.

I believe that God needed me to see and feel what it's like to have someone treat me the same way.

God didn't want to destroy me, but to make me a better man.

I believe I made each one of you feel as though you were unwanted. I made you feel unloved.

Sabina, I walked out on you and our child after saying, "I love you."

That's what I did to you and my daughter whose name I don't know.

I can't imagine the disappointment you may have felt nor the disappointment that Jesus felt and yet he still loved me.

But for the longest time I couldn't see why.

I have been praying for you both for so many years, asking that God protect you and that someday I would be able to meet you in person in order to say how sorry I am face to face.

I have missed out on so much in your lives, so much.

This is for the readers: We are all guilty of walking around thinking that we are free and clear of the things we have done in our past.

There are people that we have all hurt and never gave a second thought about them, but I am here to tell you; Jesus is saying get your life right you may never get another chance.

It's true that God forgives, but can you forget?

Reach out to those you may have offended with words or actions that caused someone hurt or pain.

How many of you are going through something right now and don't know why?

Stop for one brief second and ask God to search into your mind and your heart.

If you let Him, he will show you why.

He will let you search your heart in order for you to see the people in your life from your past you may have offended and that you have never asked for their forgiveness.

· You may have had someone reach out to you, but you said that you would never forgive them.

Think about how you felt when it happened to you and how disappointed you felt.

How hurt!

Now I need you to think about how God may be feeling.

But you can only do this through the spirit by letting Jesus into your lives.

You see God forgives us for all kinds of things we do, but we have the nerve to say to someone else, "I will never forgive you for what you did to me."

Foolish!

That's the only word I can think of is foolish.

I disappointed so many people, but lack of knowledge is no excuse.

We need to be willing to learn from our mistakes and let Jesus show us the way of making things right with those who will allow us.

Will call it the quest for forgiveness!

But first we need to make things right with God.

That's the only way anything good can come from something bad.

People you need to seek knowledge from God, asking him for wisdom on understanding.

LOVE!

This one word all by itself covers a wide area of feelings and emotions in our lives.

LOVE!

I would like to say a prayer, but before I do I'd like to say that some people say that writers write with passion.

I guess you can say that I write with a passion of love, hurt, hate, and betrayal.

You see I hated myself for hurting the one I love and by me walking away from her I betrayed not only her but the gift that God entrusted to my care.

So please forgive me.

Will you read this prayer with me?

Heavenly Father, Lord God almighty, I come to you asking that those who are reading this right now hear only your voice not my voice, not even their own voice.

I pray, Heavenly Father, that they search their hearts in order to see to whom they may have offend in their past.

Who they may have disappointed and never went to that individual and asked for forgiveness?

Maybe they had someone come to them and ask for forgiveness and instead of receiving the plea for forgiveness, because of the pain or hurt that may have built up over the years the plea was rejected.

Father God, we go around asking that you forgive us, but we have not learned how to forgive others.

So Lord I ask you to reach out to the hurt and bitter of heart and the people who have said to themselves as well as others in their lives or someone from their past that they will never forgive.

So Heavenly Father, I ask that you allow them to be given a new heart as well as a new mind.

Heavenly Father, I ask that you would also give them a new spirit in order for them to understand that Heavenly Father, you are not a God who would disappointment us.

But through our behavior and actions can we be a disappointment to you.

So, Father God, I ask in Jesus' name that you heal and restore the lost.

I would also like to add that the lost included me.

If we don't continue to seek your face, Heavenly Father, and ask each and every day for the most important thing that we need.

Love!

We will never learn to forgive or heal from hurt or disappointments that may happen more than any one given time in our lives.

Continue, Father God, to make us like Jesus and Jesus, unless you show us how to walk like you, how can we see our wrongs and not justify them as being righteous?

If we are not allowing you inside of us, how can we change?

How can we heal?

How can we forgive and embrace love once more?

If we don't stop running, how will we find you?

You have already found us.

So, with hands lifted up and with truth in your heart, close your eyes and ask Jesus to forgive you and heal your mind, spirit, and your mouth as well as your eyes because of what you have allowed others to show you in order for you to reject God in the first place.

Your mouth because of what has gone in it and in return what you have allowed to come out of it.

Your mind and spirit because of your flesh being allowed to take over which cause you to tell God, "I will change later I'm too busy having fun at this time."

Lord Jesus, we are all guilty of these things at some point in our lives.

But Heavenly Father, we must learn that because you are the truth, hope, and life but most importantly, love.

We have your forgiveness if we only ask for it and ask that you, Father, change us.

These things are only done.

Listen to me please hear me.

These things can only be done through Jesus.

So in the name of Jesus we all pray each and every day.

That you heal us from addictions that we may have found in order to release pain or hurt because we all seek healing in some way that is between you and Jesus.

Lord God, I pray that you hear every voice that cries out.

That you dry every eye that tears fall from.

Please restore the joy and take away that hate of one hating themselves that they may find forgiveness for betraying your trust.

Because of your love for us, you never stay mad. That's another reason we need to follow your footsteps.

In Jesus' name!

Amen!

In Jesus' name, amen.

Before I go any further, let's take another look at the word disappointment.

God had to deal with me because I had an issue with this word.

Only because I walked around feeling that it was okay to feel this way and I became comfortable with being disappointed and in some ways being a disappointment.

I didn't realize that this was the wrong mind set to have. People, when you walk in the path that God has set for you, you need to expect blessings, not disappointments.

But also understand that some of those things that seem like a disappointment may be a blessing in disguise in order to make you ready for the journey that lay ahead of you.

If God is taking you through something, walk it out in order to see what he has for you. Don't give up.

I'm always praying to God for wisdom.

Again, I had to learn to stop looking at God as being the reason for me feeling or thinking that because of the things I've done in my past that may not have come out to be the best decisions I may have made.

He is not a God that disappoints or casts disappointment into our lives.

Nowhere in the Bible will you find that God is a God of disappointment.

In the dictionary the word disappointment means: "To fail to satisfy the desires, hopes, or expectations of."

Even after just taking a quick glance at the meaning of the word disappointment, if you know God then you know that we all need to repent for even feeling that he is responsible for anything like that in our lives.

The Bible says that when he looked upon the earth, he could not find one not one who was free from sin.

But instead of destroying us all, what did he do? He sent Jesus.

Because of our disappointment to him, he decided to give us another chance so that our sins and disappointments to him may be forgiven.

God did something for us that we ourselves find it so hard to do and follow it all the way through; He sacrificed Jesus His son.

Not saying that anyone should try or do this, you're not God and they are not Jesus.

In doing that, there is no selfishness, hatred, nor are there any ulterior motives behind that which was given.

Life!

As well as the greatest showing of love.

Yet we find it hard to sacrifice ourselves for life in Heaven.

Wow!

There was no trickery behind what God did nor was there any trickery in what Jesus did.

We were bought with a price and all we are being asked is to give our life to Jesus in order to receive a gift like no other.

That gift is God's heavenly kingdom.

Like I said, I used to sit and think that because of the way that I hurt people in the past that this was a form of disappointment and it is, but I used to think that I suffered disappointments in my life and that was God's way of dealing with me.

But you have to look at it this way; if that was so of God, then the sacrifice of Jesus was for nothing.

It would have all been a lie.

When I was in the world, that was a way of life because the Devil is a god of lies and disappointment.

But the choices I made were mine.

But his job is to make us believe that this is something of God.

There are so many people who are walking around feeling lost every day and believing that all life has to offer is disappointment, but I am here to tell you that is not the case.

I had to stop running from who Jesus was in my life as well as what he wanted for my life.

It has not been enjoyable.

Meaning some of the things I had to face about myself.

When God shows you your faults, it's not easy to face, but you can only see if you are truly willing to look and not turn away from what you see.

He will show you your shame.

It has not been without pain and tears as well as confusion.

But it has been with a lot of asking Jesus for strength and asking Him to go before the Father on my behalf.

You see, otherwise I would not have had the strength on my own to do what it takes to survive.

I am still going through in this walk with my Heavenly Father Jehovah as well as my Lord and Savior Jesus Christ.

Satan will tug and pull and fill your mind and spirit with lies and disappointments.

While God is trying to make the changes in you in order to receive that which he has promised you, stop looking at God the way Satan wants you to see him.

But first, ask Jesus to show you who Satan really is and what he is out to do in the world, your world.

When you do, you will find peace in a way that in order to know that you are in such a place someone else would need to tell you because only through the eyes of others can it be seen.

But you also have to watch out for the person who is telling you because a friend may not be a friend, a brother or sister may not be who they say they are. I had to find out the hard way on that matter.

You are the one who allows someone to come into your life.

Do you remember that man or that woman you meet and they became your husband or wife?

When you meet them, you allowed them into your life and for most of us we thought we found the person that would be there for life.

{We will get back to this subject later in the book}

Nowadays I ask God to show me who someone truly is between two to three days if they are for me or against me.

The most important thing is if they have been sent by him to be a part of his will that needs to be done in my life or yours.

I know that I have had angels come through and speck to me and reveal things that are going to take place in my life.

I have also had demons come and try to take me off course and in one of those ways through the word disappointment because that was what I started to really believe.

I believed that I was to get used to having nothing but disappointments in my life.

That this was how my life would continue to go on, nothing would change or get better for me at any point of my life.

This is how Satan gets in and causes us to make the wrong chooses and instead of running to Jesus we run away and chase after what he is offering us instead of that which God has already promised would be ours.

Only we don't want the pain and the suffering or have to go through the waiting stage that God puts in place in order to make us ready for the gifts that he has in store for us.

Did you know that there are two different types of withdraw?

The greatest withdraw that God has is that which involves withdrawing of the world and letting go of the worldly things.

We will fight against letting go of hurt, pain, greed and lust; this is just to name a few.

The one thing that Satan wants you to run from is love, joy, peace, and truth just to name a few.

So instead Satan says, "I will give to you whatever you want right here and now, just forsake God and your life with him and live the life he has for you and all the things that you desire will be yours. Oh yeah, don't worry, you will still make it in to Heaven."

But you see he will give you the things you want, but you will still deal with the feelings of the world.

He is right, you will make it into what he calls Heaven and what Jesus calls Hell. Wake up please!

I fear that there are already so many souls about to be lost forever therefore do you not realize it's so dangerous to wait one more second.

Jesus is the way to the Father. We must go through him and repent and give our lives back to him.

Hasn't the pain of the world been enough for you?

Stop running from Jesus.

Do you remember praying to God for those changes in you and in someone else?

Was it that you wanted them to change to be a better person or to be the person you wanted them to be?

Did you want them to walk more like Jesus or more like someone else you had your eyes on?

When Jesus begins the healing process that's when you stop and want to run away because of the pain you are going to have to take on, but you have to learn to face the pain. It only lasts for a while.

When God had to give up Jesus for our sins, think how much that hurt him, knowing that he could have stopped it all and said, "My son is not worth a world of people who do not love or respect me. I'll just let them all die."

But he said, "No, I will show them that love and sacrifice are the key words I need them to understand because that's what God used to save us."

Jesus could have chosen not to go through with giving his life for us. But he said, "Father, let your will be done."

So, I say to you go before the Father and say, "Lord, let your will be done in my life."

But when you do, grab on to Jesus with one hand and God with the other and never let go.

Ask that they never let go of you.

This I pray in Jesus mighty name. Amen.

Remember when Jesus said, "Father, forgive them for they know not what they do"? 1I this time that we live in there are no excuses.

Because we have the Bible, as well as prayer.

If someone is on your mind from your past that you may have hurt or disappointed or rejected a plea for forgiveness, it could be God saying reach out to those individuals in order to set your spirit free.

Turn that word of disappointment into hope that a greater change is coming in your life. Walk through life waiting on the blessing of the Lord.

But remember it may not come when you want it, but it will be on time, God's time.

One important thing I must also tell you is that you have to want and believe that the things you ask God for you shall receive because doubt in your mind and heart it shows that you have no faith in Jesus.

It also shows that you don't believe that whatever you have or are going through God can fix it.

Can I ask you a question and that is, would you believe a friend or family member before you would believe God?

Would you take their advice or the word of Jesus?

Would you thank them or yourself for something that God did in your life?

I walked around for the longest time feeling like I was in complete darkness I could not see any light at all.

I had begun to feel like God would never forgive me, so I know what a lot of you may be feeling, but again don't run away, run into the arms of Jesus he will change the lie of not being able to be forgiven.

To telling you the truth, there is nothing too great for our God and that he already knew what was going to happen in your life before your life even began.

So, forgiveness was already there.

Smiles...

What we fail to realize is whatever desires that lay inside of one's heart or mind will manifest themselves as temptations in that person's life.

There are people who at one time do not know who they were even when they look in the mirror.

They drift into another dimension and gave into their temptation. Lust, greed, pride, and hate are just examples.

The question is why?

When they return to reality, they were not the same.

The answer is that they allowed themselves to be tempted and they gave into the temptation. Afterwards, they began to remember who they actually were.

They disappeared into another realm and had to catch up to the real time upon return.

Often times they did not recognize some of the choices they made or who they had become at that time.

Chapter 4

The lesson in patience, can it lead to doubt?

When it comes to the nature of developing true patience, it truly is a test of your faith.

When life itself feels like your world is falling down all around you and it seems like your all alone with no one to help you, what do you do?

What or who do you turn to for help?

When you seem to have everyone around you saying, "I am praying for you," how do you feel?

When you know what's going on in your life.

But everyone around you has no idea or any understanding.

How do you deal with what they are saying and what you are dealing with in your life?

Sometimes it feels like you leave out of the house with an empty bowl and expected it to be full by the time you return back home again.

Yet it's still empty.

Do you and can you still trust in Jesus?

Can you still be patient because the Bible says weeping may endure for a night, but joy cometh in the morning?

Only it seems like you have been weeping for so long, you begin to ask God the question, 'How long before the joy you said I would have will come?"

But the Lord says he is an on-time God. They that wait on the Lord shall.

That word shall is for you to answer for yourself what it is that you are wanting and waiting for from Jesus to do in your life.

I would like to start this chapter off by asking you this question. When God is taking you through the restructuring of your spirit, mind, body, and soul, have you noticed that he put you in a place where it seems as though no one excess but you?

In 2nd Corinthians 12:9, "And he said unto me, my grace is sufficient for thee; for my strength is made perfect in weakness."

Most gladly therefore will I rather glory in my infirmities, that the power of Christ may rest upon me.

Infirmity means: physical or mental weakness.

Let's add spiritual disability or lacking of power.

We begin to have a lack of power and a disability of the spirit because we will not allow the power of Christ to rest upon us.

Again, God says for His strength is made perfect in our weakness.

For his grace is sufficient for thee.

If we look at the scripture Deuteronomy 8:2, "And thou shalt remember all the ways which the Lord thy God led thee these forty years in the wilderness to humble thee and to prove thee to know what was in thine heart, whether thou wouldest keep his commandments or not."

You look around and your whole life has changed nothing is the same even down to the people in your past life.

But in this new world the Lord has taken you too or shall we say a new level of training.

God has also taken you to a place that he needs you to be in order for you to get to know his will in your life he has also taken you to a new realm.

It appears that this place is worse than where you were before and no matter what you do you just can't see a way out.

You being to see others being blessed and you start to ask Jesus if there is something that you are doing wrong.

Everyone around me is being blessed.

GOING FROM AN ANGRY MAN TO A PEACEFUL MAN
IS NOT AN EASY JOURNEY

It seems as though no one cares or can hear what you feel inside, you feel you want to run but there is nowhere to go.

Trapped!

You feel like you're not alive because people seem to not notice or pay you any mind.

You want love but it seems as though when people look at you, they look at you with disgust.

I have also found that when you don't have anything to offer anyone who has never been without you don't matter you become invisible.

Even the so-called respect that someone may have had for you is lost.

We talk about respect of person, it's not the person we respect but what that person has to offer.

These things take place in our lives, our homes, and even in the church.

Now when God is taking us through the process of chastening it's so that he can take you and allow you to see the mistakes that you made in your past.

Sometimes he has to do this through teaching one how to have patience because there maybe something going on in your life that only through patience can the truth or answer be provided to you.

You see God wants you to be able to see things that you have never been able to see with the eyes of the flesh.

Sometimes that trap you may feel you're in may have been a blessing.

But then sometimes that blessing you feel may just be a trap.

When it comes to life, we are to live to love and love to live.

If we follow the will of God, this takes place in our lives every day.

When we get married, there are times when the marriage is over.

Jesus was trying to teach me how to see, hear, and understand the signs.

When two people become strangers to each other in marriage.

What we didn't realize is how long had we become strangers to each other.

But the most important question is, how long has this been going on in our lives?

But even through all that, I thank God for the peace he had placed in my heart as well as the love in my spirit.

49

Sometimes I don't know if it's harder to let someone that you love go.

Or if it's harder to love the one you hate if you still love them.

Sometimes you stay with someone and you are just there while the one you're with is wondering why you're there because your spirit left a long time ago.

The word "patient" means: demonstrating uncomplaining endurance under distress.

Now during a period of time God was having me continuously reaching out to my ex-wife I felt like a fool.

I began to talk with the Lord saying, "Father God, she only rejects me."

He then said, "Are you still able to love her even when she rejects you?" and I said, "Yes."

He then asked me, "Is there great pain in your spirit?"

I said, "Yes."

But then I did not hear anything else.

Silence.

This went on for some time.

I began to worry that I had done something wrong.

I began to wonder if the woman I was married to ever really loved me, also if I really knew her at all.

But then Jesus said to me the rejection you felt and the pain that you are feeling you had to go through it in order to understand how it makes me and my Father feel when it's done to us.

What people seem to forget is that we have feelings not like that of a human, but nonetheless we do

Why do you think God gave Jesus as a sacrifice if he did not have feelings and did not care for you or me?

One thing is he knows when you have stopped loving him, yet he keeps on loving you.

Both the Father and the son and the Holy Spirit.

How many of you have felt or have gone through a similar situation?

There was so much that I had to learn through dealing with having to be patient.

GOING FROM AN ANGRY MAN TO A PEACEFUL MAN
IS NOT AN EASY JOURNEY

I had to learn to be patient with love as well as life.

I had to learn to have patience in order to let go of the hate in order for love to reside in my spirit.

When someone hurts you, the first thing you want to do is to be angry with them.

God began to show me that it's hard for a person to be angry with themselves for the things that they did.

It's even harder for them to say to themselves or to another it could have been something I did as well.

The reason being is because of the choices that they and even myself made.

Instead of facing ourselves, we decided to hurt the one's we loved.

Past hurts, if not dealt with, can be a danger to any new relationship.

I had to learn that I had lived with so much hate in my life growing up that I didn't want that type of life anymore.

When it affected my marriage, I knew I had to change.

I wanted the hurt to stop, so I began to pray and ask God to change me from the inside out.

It seemed as though I couldn't get through to God or Jesus.

I began to hurt in a way that my body began to hurt on the inside.

Like my ribs were breaking and my lungs collapsing.

It was hard to stand because my legs were weak.

My body filled with tears that I never thought would stop flowing.

The tears began to fall and I felt that something was wrong with me because I could not stop hurting nor could I stop crying.

I had to stay away from people because I continued to cry but I could not understand what was going on with me.

My ex and I both become so disrespectful to each other during our marriage and when she filed for the divorce that was God's way of setting us free, but I did not know it at the time.

The divorce was done with an e-mail. You seem after being notified in that manner, I had gotten to the point that I was not going to disrespect another person again and I was not going to allow anyone to disrespect me as well.

Now I had no idea that God was working on me in order to be able to let her go finally.

Because the flesh is what we have to fight when letting go of hate, but the spirit is what we deal with when letting go of love.

When love is gone, even though it's dead, the nerve is still a live until it too dies.

One of the things I started asking God to do was reveal the truth to me about myself and my feelings.

I also asked Jesus to show me the feelings of those around me so that I would know who I need to let into my life and who I needed to let go.

It's sad that someone will try to mess with your feelings by playing games with your heart.

Some people feel that they are great actresses or actors, but their acting coach can't compete with mine.

My teacher of life began to show me how to watch what was going on how to see how they start off acting nice towards you.

Ah.

They now have your guard down by sweet talking you.

They begin to say to themselves he or she seems happy now it's time to hurt them again.

They begin to ask you to do things but as soon as you stop or slow down.

It's time to leave and find someone else.

Now is this true?

That the devil puts things in our minds.

But then we apply it to our lives.

You see, we have things that are bottled up inside and at some point, in our lives it may come to surface.

The people or person I'm talking about is me and you.

We can become that person who wants to hurt the other someone else because we have been hurt or used by someone in our past.

Instead of blaming ourselves, we want to blame the devil and say he put voices in our head, but that voice is yours because of anger or hate.

Most of you thought that I was going to say the other person or yes, it's true only I would be telling a lie.

I remember visiting some friends and as I watched them and how they began to show their love to one another.

I began to see how my marriage was and I began to say to myself that's not the type of marriage I want or wanted.

I never want to go through being married to a stranger again.

A loveless and a disrespectful marriage.

You can never please someone who does not want to be happy.

In Romans 8:5 it says, "Those who live according to the sinful nature have their minds set on what that nature desires; but those who live in accordance with the spirit have their minds set on what the spirit desires."

Sometimes we can set our own selves up into thinking that someone is truly meant to be in our lives that we put a false elusion in our own spirit.

God knows that your love is true that's why he has to teach you with patients how to let go so that you move on in victory.

One of the greatest strengths is love, but the hardest is when you have to let go and move on.

Have you ever been in a relationship that did not seem to be working the way you thought?

It could be a marriage or friendship.

So, you begin talking to different people who are giving you bad advice and you become confused on what to do.

They say "Leave! Move on!"

Isn't that what people say?

Do you believe that someone who care about your relationship would tell you to just move on?

What ever happen to talking to people who would sit and talk with you and then ask the question.

Do you feel there is a chance that neither one of you are given this relationship all that you have or are you going on the opinions of others?

We have moved away from hearing each other instead we harden our hearts towards each other and only hear people outside saying leave.

Do you know that's how we do Jesus?

These people begin to tell you things that are not from God, but you have set your own selves up after that by reacting in a negative way, and they begin to say.

The Lord has someone better for you so you begin to do everything in your power to break up the trust in the relationship.

You begin to see things going on that is not really there and hear things that make you feel good because it's coming from someone who is only telling you what you want to hear.

This is because most people prefer to live a life of pleasure and lies.

But for the ones who face the truth and close their ears to lies who seek and find God.

In 1 Corinthians 14: 33, it says, "For God is not the author of confusion but of peace."

Could this be happening to you or has it happened?

There are times when we know we should walk away.

But it's not our friends we turn to we have a habit of turning to a complete stranger that we should turn away from.

But if we turn to a friend and they begin to tell us the truth about ourselves we can't except that, it's not what we want to hear.

When you turn to the lord, he helps to strengthen you by allowing you to hear the truth and to embraces it, so once the Lord reveals the truth.

When you are approach by those who are trying to drive you away from the one you love turn and run away.

But for you, others who have been listening to what God says in his word.

Psalms 27:14 says, "Wait on the Lord; Be of good courage, And He shall strengthen your heart; Wait, I say, on the Lord!"

There have been so many wrong decisions that I have made growing up.

I had people that talked to me.

If I had the people that were a part of my life talk with me on a level of being on both our sides, not just listening to one person but us both that could have turned my life around or if I knew the things I know now, it may have not change anything, the reason being God would have still had me here in order for me to share with you what Jesus is doing in my spirit not then but now.

But please don't get me wrong, I still make bad decisions, but Jesus shows me when I do and is here to help me get back on track.

He has placed me with people who love and care when my peace is disturbed.

We know the flesh is real and our minds, if we allow, can be persuaded to turn for good to living a life of confusion which leads to making wrong decisions.

What a lot of people don't realize is that the dogs that God placed in my life have helped me so much in this walk and in understanding that love does not stop and does not walk out on you if treated with love.

This is also how we must find ourselves in our relationships with Jesus and with the people who are placed in our lives.

Learn to be patient, first starting with yourself and then with your husbands, wives, children, and friends.

But Jesus is the way to understanding and learning patience and how to gain control over you.

It all starts within, inside of you and inside of me.

God is in control, but you have to let go and give it to Him; meaning your will and flesh. Give it to Him before it's too late.

Did you know that patience in the dictionary is "the capacity to accept or tolerate delay, trouble, or suffering without getting angry or upset"?

God teaches us how to deal with the endurance of difficult circumstances.

These difficulties deal with the trials of change.

Going from the way of the world to the way that God is now leading you towards your new life with him.

Through patience, Jesus shows us how to accept or tolerate delay and to not react when trouble and suffering comes our way without getting angry or upset.

Learning to find love and peace in every circumstance.

In 1 Thessalonians: 5:18 it says, "Give thanks in all circumstances; for this is God's will for you in Christ Jesus."

Did you know that some people never recover from something like losing a spouse or loved one, a child?

Now in this case we are not talking about the death of a loved one as far as death of spirit.

This deals with someone who was never truly in your life.

Just pretending, waiting for the perfect time to rip your heart out, but they had to be patient in their wrong doing.

I need you to realize that patience can be used for good and bad.

You see how could you lose someone who was never there in the first place; you can't lose what you never had.

God will allow so many different avenues to be made available to someone when he is trying to get them to get back on the right path.

But sometimes either the lust of the flesh or something that we feel we can't wait on because we have to have it now will change your life!

We can develop a hate aimed towards ourselves that will prevent and not allow us to see or hear what God is trying to do or say.

I know this to be fact because that was how I became a bitter man more than one time in my life.

Sometimes we do so much damage within ourselves that because of that damage we can't forgive and it's not forgiving the other person, it's forgiving ourselves.

I have to say that I thank God for my two dogs because they have been like two angels watching over me.

It's amazing how God has allowed me to be an angel to watch over them.

When we were sick, God took care of us.

When we were in need, God provided for us.

I want to share with you a situation that we were placed in and at the time I could not see what was about to happen or away out.

After my life began to crumble before my eyes, me and the dogs moved to Stone Mountain and after moving from the place we had stayed for a while we moved into another place.

Now, when we first moved there the landlord said he was working on the house so me and the dogs had the whole house to ourselves.

But as time went on, things got bad.

I was paying my rent to the landlord and sometimes he would pay the light bill on time. Sometimes he would pay it late and the electricity would get cut off.

Even though I was paying the rent on time, he took advantage of the situation I was in at the time.

I had to have somewhere that would allow my dogs to be with me.

I remember he started renting out rooms and because he would get mad at someone or someone did not pay their rent, he would take it out on everyone staying there.

Lights would be cut off, the cable, sometimes even the water.

I would pray and ask God, "Why is this happening to me?"

I remember there was this gay couple, two males, and a dog that had moved into the room across from mine.

One of them was still at work and the other was at home drinking and had been talking to someone on the phone all day.

Once the other guy got home, they began to shout and to argue and it got louder and my dogs started to bark because they were fighting.

You then heard them come out of their room and go into the kitchen. The yelling continued, so I went to see what was going on because their dog was yelping and to my surprise the one guy was stabbing the dog.

The dog ran by me into their room crying and then the one who stabbed the dog went after the other guy and stabbed him straight through the arm with a ten inch steak knife.

He had a steak knife in one hand and a fork knife used for the grill in the other hand and he then stabbed him in the back with the steak knife.

I then yelled out, "It's not worth it. Please stop, you don't need to do this."

I keep my distance, one for the blood and the other because I did not want to be hurt.

The one who did the stabbing began to say why, why he gave me Aids he knew he had it why did he give it to me.

When the police came, they got the dog and he died on the table at the vet.

But the dog ran to the one he thought was going to protect him and instead he was the one who killed him.

The one who did the stabbing was caught a few blocks away.

One questions when will we be humans first.

I had to set in a police car in the back set for two and a half hours and when I asked, "Why are you treating me like I did something wrong?" I was told that, "We have to do this because sometimes our witnesses leave."

To me, I was not treated as a witness or a human being. It was hot outside and they just had the widow cracked.

I was made to feel like an animal in a cage.

Can you tell me why?

Has anything happened to you like this or anyone you know?

Work with us and we can learn to trust and work with you.

Can I just be real? Every time I get pulled over, I have to pray to Jesus before the police officer reaches my car because I don't know how his/her day has gone.

I don't know what kind of mind frame they are in at that moment.

They may be police officers, but they are still living and breathing flesh and blood who also have bad days and can take it out on someone else.

Just keeping it real!

After all that I was going through with the land lord and that situation, I began to pray even the more, asking God to get us away from this mess that was going on.

I remember one day during the summer I got a call from one of the other tenants in the house that the land lord did not pay the light bill so there was no AC going in the house and my dogs were yelping.

I had to leave work and he then threatened me saying he was going to call animal control on me.

Thank God I was able to take them to work with me. It was on a Thursday and after I got off, we went and looked at a place in Lawrenceville, GA. I packed up that Friday and we were gone.

But I did not see away out, even when Jesus was moving in my behalf.

My faith and our lives had been put to the test not to see us fail but to help us to rise and gain strength through our trials and to realize when you trust in Jesus you're a winner even when you can't see it at the time.

I'm not saying it easy, because it's not. It's not!

While trying to get the first book completed, I was without a job after the book went on sale. I was still unemployed.

I was even taken advantage of by the company I used to publish the book for me.

That hit me hard and I started to believe the negative talk from people who wanted me to fell.

The pain set in and I began to feel like a failure.

Jesus had to open my eyes as well as my spirit in order for me to begin to see things in a different light.

Jesus then said to me, "Do you want the riches of the word?"

If your answer is "no," allow me to be blessed by way of the riches from my Father's kingdom which is in his word.

People see you as having nothing, but through your faith and allowing my Father which art in Heaven to supply all your needs, I know you try to walk as I did and yet you stumble and fall.

Because you see what others have and what you have not.

What matters is that you do what is asked and you have done it with your heart wide open even while you were dealing with so much pain.

Greater is the reward to he who waits on the Lord then he who tries to get that which was never meant for them to have.

The Lord began to show that the money for the book was not what he wanted me to have, but to learn how to deal and grow from disappointment and how to put it to good use.

Sometimes we are given a chance to make a new start when things go wrong.

So, what I decide to do from this point on dealing with disappointment is how I deal with it in a positive way and that will determine my life from here on out.

I know that when Jesus showed me what was taking place in my life, I began to walk around saying I am what God say's I am.

I can do what God says I can do.

Most people began to question and ask why is he not feeling down anymore.

He has no money. He's a loser.

They could not see what I could see and that was how God was making me a winner.

God was now teaching me how to gain the victory.

Now during the process of writing the first book I went through a lot of crying because of the pain I was feeling and after praying it seemed like nothing was getting better.

This went on for over three years and I began to say, "Lord, I don't want to cry anymore I don't want to feel any more pain."

I began to pray to God about seeking the truth about my feelings and I wanted to seek the truth about others and their feelings towards me.

Heavenly Father, I seek the truth about the people that are in my life as well as the people that are surrounding me and the ones that need not be a part of my life.

Heavenly Father, the most important thing is that I seek your love your strength and your joy also your peace.

I can live my life without anyone being in it but I can't live without you.

He then said to me, "Without pain, how can you grow closer to me? Without pain, how can you gain strength? Without pain, how do you know if you are alive? How can you help others if you don't know what they are going through? Just as Jesus had to come to earth to know what to do to help you deal with the pain, you're going through so that you gain the victory not death by way of going to Hell."

Through the process of learning patience, He gave me strength so that this time I was able to walk away and say enough is enough.

I don't want my joy stolen anymore. I don't want my spirit filled with confusion anymore.

I don't want my spirit chasing after death because that's where I would be headed.

GOING FROM AN ANGRY MAN TO A PEACEFUL MAN
IS NOT AN EASY JOURNEY

For those of you who are out there who feel that you can't let go of the person that is not there for you anymore, that husband, that wife, even that girlfriend or boyfriend. Just keeping it real so I have to put it out there with that too.

Just knew that through patience, prayer, and determination, most of all through God's will that he will carry you through.

This also applies to people with addictions.

It's not easy to let go, but it can be done through our Lord Jesus.

Please let Him help you.

Let go of the world it won't last.

You're not alone in how you feel.

Sometimes you feel foolish about how your feeling because you love someone and your praying to mend your marriage or relationship only sometimes it doesn't work out that way.

The Bible says our way of thinking may not be what God has planned for us.

Sometimes that other person is praying for someone else to be in their lives.

They say a house divided cannot stand.

God allowed everything that did not matter to be taken out of my life in order to show me that I only need Him. That is the greatest need in my life.

Jesus!

The most important thing I have to say to everyone who is reading this is even though it seems like a rough ride in life with everything you may be going through, things such as people walking out on you that you love.

You may have lost your job your home and it just keeps getting worse and nothing seems to be looking up for you, just know that if you have not given up on God, he will not give up on you.

I need you to know what Hebrews 12: 1 says, "Therefore we also, since we are surrounded by so great a cloud of witnesses, let us lay aside every weight, and the sin which so easily ensnares us, and let us run with endurance the race that is set before us."

While I was thinking that I lost everything, what was actually taken place was I was moving into a greater relationship and covenant with our Heavenly Father, our Lord Jesus, and the Holy Spirit.

At one point in our lives, we had role models and mentors that one could look up to that wanted to teach us the right way of living God's way even if they themselves did not believe in Jesus.

In James 3: 16-18 it says, "For where envy and self-seeking exist, confusion and every evil thing are there. But the wisdom that is from above is first pure, then peaceable, gentle, willing to yield, full of mercy and good fruits, without partiality and without hypocrisy."

Now the fruit of righteousness is sown in peace by those who make peace.

Today, right now, people, our children and teens, are following mentors and role models who are teaching them how to make fast, illegal money.

Who can sleep with the most men and women?

Who can kill the most people?

They do everything negative even though the price they will pay will be a great price in which no peace will ever be found.

In 2 Timothy 3: 2-7 it says, "For men will be lovers of themselves, lovers of money, boasters, proud, blasphemers, disobedient to parents. unthankful, unholy, unloving, unforgiving, slanderers, without self-control, brutal, despisers of good, traitors, headstrong, haughty, lovers of pleasure rather than lovers of God, having a form of godliness but denying its power."

And from such people turn away!

For of this sort are those who creep into households and make captives of gullible women and men loaded down with sins, led away by various lusts, always learning and never able to come to the knowledge of the truth.

In 1 Peter 2: 11 it says, "Beloved, I beg you as so journeyers and pilgrims, abstain from fleshly lusts which war against the soul."

It's not an easy thing to do alone. That's why we need Jesus.

So just know that sometimes you have to let go of the world in order for God to take you where you need to be for Him.

Even though you may have lost the ones you love and they hurt and keep rejecting you, God has not rejected or turned his back on you.

Remember when I said that God asked me the question, "When you are being rejected by your wife or husband even friends does it cause pain to your spirit?"

I said, "yes."

He then said, "Do you still love her/them?" and I said, "yes."

He then said, "That was what I needed to teach you and that is no matter what someone does to you, never stop loving and praying for them."

He then said, "That this is how I love you when you rejected me and caused me pain yet I still love you. I will always love you."

So don't keep chasing after those who don't want to be caught by you anymore. Chase after the one who wants you to embrace him and he will embrace you back forever and he will always be faithful and will never let you down.

Jesus will lead the one into your life that will bring happiness and joy in the mate you deserve because sometimes we want to go after a desire or lust for the one we feel is the one we need.

Only Jesus wants to give you the love that will last not lust that will only be but a brief moment it just maybe away to save your life not give it away.

Smile.

God is saying, "My sons and daughters, why are you letting yourselves be dragged down?"

You may not notice the changes that may be taking place, but Jesus is saying, "Open your eyes. Hear my voice."

He will show you if you allow him what is going on and how you are slowly allowing yourselves to go right back to that trap that God took you from.

You'll start to notice that you're getting a little moody and your beginning to become a little drawn back.

Stop!

Please listen to Jesus. We're talking about your soul, it's not a game, so stop treating it as though it is. Please!

Sometimes we have to ask God, "How do I not stop loving them?" but He'll say, "Don't, but here is the strength to walk away while in your right mind and spirit."

There are a lot of people that can't say that because they refuse to let go.

I really thought that was how my life was going to go not being able to let go, but I let God and he gave me strength to let go.

Just as he did for me, he is able to do the same for you, but you have to let Him be the blessing in order to be blessed.

Until God began talking to me and showing me things that no one else knew I did not know if I was going to make it.

You see I had no job, no car. I was lonely and alone. I felt as though I did not exist, that I wasn't alive.

I know there are many who feel the same. You feel as though you're not alive, but you are, it's just that you're being reborn and now you have to start all over again with things such as learning how to walk and how to talk all over again as a child.

You have to learn how to notice right from wrong all over again, not through the flesh, but through the spirit.

You're not living your life anymore through the flesh, so you will not feel the same or have the same people in your life.

Satan knows how true and strong your love was for that man or that woman, so he had to teach them to run from you and reject you otherwise he wouldn't win their soul, But also because of the love you had for that person. He wanted you to love them more than God.

This way you would walk away from the will and protection of God.

The one thing we need to realize that sometimes they don't come back and it's okay. Continue to love them and pray for them, but love yourself and keep moving. Don't look back, keep looking toward Heaven and Jesus will fill all voids in your life.

Have you ever truly had peace during the storms of life?

All I can do is take a deep breath and say it feels good even to have love when those that used to be in your life stopped loving you.

No matter what went wrong, you need not feel that you were to blame.

It doesn't mean that it was your fault or that something was wrong with you.

It could have been something in them or just something that needed to take place so that the voice of God could be heard so that they could make the choice of who they would like to follow.

Ask yourself this question: Who do you look at as your God?

GOING FROM AN ANGRY MAN TO A PEACEFUL MAN
IS NOT AN EASY JOURNEY

Remember, sometimes when we feel like we need to run away or we can't let go, it may be something inside of us.

Fear of loving someone or fear of being alone.

Which one of these apply to you and how you're living your life?

Chapter 5

The last kiss good-bye the story begins

Lord, why do the ones I love make me feel like I'm not important in their life anymore?

This is something I have been dealing with for a long time.

Wow!

I could only continue to ask myself what am I to do because I don't know.

How many of you have asked God this question and then said words similar to these?

Heavenly Father, I know you said you would not put more on me then I can bear.

How can I be the husband/wife, father/mother, sister/brother, or family member that they need me to be?

How can I be some kind of rock of security that makes them feel they are needed when I feel as if I have already lost them.

I have pleaded the blood of Jesus over marriages/relationships, family members, and friends. You have shown me visions.

Jesus, what must I do?

This was what I would pray when I was going through the pain of walking out on my first family.

When I was praying about the marriage, I was in God showed me after time went by that it was not me.

I remember I was praying so hard this one time before she life for the last time.

I heard a voice say to me that in two weeks she is going to leave. Only this time, do not chase after her. There is a path that she must go down that does not include you.

Like most of you I said, "Father, this is my wife! What do you mean do not chase after her?"

"My son, you have been doing what I have ask of you in showing your love for her, so now show your love for me by doing as I am asking of you now."

When that was said, I began to ask the Lord with all of the things that I was doing wrong how was I showing love.

He then said, "With all of the pain and suffering, you were still seeking me for change."

If you didn't have love you would not have wanted to change for love.

With tears in my eyes I ask why my life has been turned upside down.

You have showed me how to love this woman but not how to stop.

Why did I hurt her when all I want to do is love her?

Please Father God, help me. I don't understand.

Help me.

How can I just let her go?

"My son, if you look at what is going on around you, she has already let you go. Remember her last words were remember the kiss you got that was the last kiss you will ever have from me and your keys are in the door."

The last kiss goodbye.

You have become lost by the way you're showing your determination to show how much you love her that you cannot hear my voice only the sound of your own.

Jesus, I just want to be able to give her the love you are teaching me to have for her.

The love I am teaching you to have is not just for her alone, but for yourself as well as those around you.

No matter who the person, maybe, or what that person may do to you, I don't want anything to make you want to feel any other way.

Love them!

Then walk away and let me heal you.

Have you ever been so lost in your own thoughts that you sometimes think you hear one thing, only to realize that something else was being said?

This is what took place with me. You see, God told me that my ex-wife was going to leave. That's what took place.

He also said not to chase after her.

But the thing is I thought the Lord told me that there was a road that she had to travel that did not include me, but it was the other way around it was me that would travel a path that even I had no idea what this journey would include or if I would be able to survive.

At some point in your life has God ever told you not to chase after someone because you can't catch what has already gone away?

As well as when you try to catch the wind the more you try to catch it the more your mind will you allow to fool yourself into thinking that it is something that can be caught.

It hurt to receive that text from her, but I know that there was nothing that I could do. She was a grown woman and would do what she wanted no matter what I said anyway.

She had stopped hearing my voice, but I am not sure if she ever heard my voice at all.

When did we stop caring for the lost and broken hearted and those whose spirits are lost and confused?

What has happened to seeking the lost and broken hearted as well as the spirit?

When did we stop going out to reach and re-teach the ones who have fallen along the way?

If one strays, we go after that one.

Either we are to wrapped up with ourselves or pretend that we have no time for anyone else because we are so wrapped up in church work or our own self being.

The devil wants to divide the family, but it's us who go around destroying our relationships.

People who are supposed to help sometimes kill what was had between two people.

That's what is happing to day in life.

I had the chance to talk with a young lady, her name is Malissa.

She shared with me that peer pressure doesn't only come from friends, other teens, or children, but from people who call themselves adults or leaders who are supposed to help in their growth process.

Sometimes because of the way a child my dress we tend to label them with words that are unkind and that may do more harm than good.

They are told that they will never become anything or that all they will do is make babies and not become nothing else, but baby makers and become lazy.

They are told they are headed down a road that will lead them straight to jail. All this just by looking at someone.

Being told by teachers and others that their stupid because of the people they hang around not understanding that they are some of the smartest in the class.

When will we stop looking at the outside of a person and look on the inside?

We need to sit and talk with our youth and listen sometimes without saying a word.

They are becoming afraid to want to move ahead because they feel they are not heard nor are they seen.

There are so many people who don't know where to turn anymore because people are more likely to turn up their nose and roll their eyes at them.

Sometimes to say, "Hello," people look at you as to say, "Leave me alone" or "Can I help you?" All with attitude.

Where are you getting your training from and whose voice are you hearing?

We are supposed to be hearing God and learning his ways, but what has happened to love?

What happened to blessing someone with a smile even if you're having a bad day and seeing how it will make your day even greater?

Try it and see for yourself.

There are so many people who instead of living there on lives and seeing what they have will kiss it all away with stories they heard others tell.

You go out with your friends and you sit around seeing who can tell the greats stories dealing with their life.

Yet as you tell your own and you add a little here and take away a little there because you want to come out as the one that all are looking at as having their life together.

You forget about your own lies that had been told in order to fit in even though your life is not going well.

You begin to hear the stories that the others told and the lies you told and become lost in those lies.

You can't see that all that talk has blinded you into believing the stories about your great life and how much you wanted what the others had you start believing and wanting things to be true.

Or it may be that God is blessing you, but it's not coming fast enough for you so you decide to take matters into your own hands.

Why are so many people wanting to live someone else's life instead of their own?

Why is it that when it comes to going to church, wives get mad at their husbands and tell them they need to act more like the pastor?

They forget that you're the man/woman to whom they married, not the pastor or any other man/woman, but you.

Husbands get mad and tell the wives, "Why do you always want to fuss and fight?" and then they just pick some woman's name and most of the time it's one of her friends and then say, "Why can't you be like her?"

The thing of it is that you may both be listening to some of the same people giving false stories and tell you both separate lies.

People stop believing that people live a perfect life without dealing with something that may off set their marriage at times.

But learn to live your life and stop taking and wanting someone else's.

If you act like you don't understand, husbands, leave someone else's wife alone.

Wives, leave another woman's husband alone.

If you're not happy with your marriage, don't break up someone else's marriage.

If you can't listen to each other, if you're having problems, why are you allowing yourself to listen to anyone else trying to give you advice?

In order to make a marriage or relationship work you first must be willing to hear each other, before the voices of those you had been telling your flesh stories to which now you began to close your spirit so that now you can't even hear the voice of God.

A lot of people say they go to Jesus and pray and ask for help.

My question is, do you?

Is it that you pray blaming the other person never including yourself?

So instead of being happy with who you're with, you listen to other people on how their life is going and then you start telling yourself that's what I want.

You begin what I call the downward spiral of the last kiss good-bye.

All of a sudden, they begin to try to change their partner into someone they're not and then begin to go around sleeping with others in order to try to find what they already have.

In the Bible it says that God created the world with a word and it was done and he was glad with it.

We do the same thing when we destroy something that God may have put together.

We destroy it with a word.

How many of you have just said, "Lord I give up, I am defeated, I can't deal with this no more"?

Try this before you leave your house look in the mirror and say to yourself, "Today is a blessed day and God has blessed me."

When you leave out of your house and everyone you come into contact with say to them with a smile, "You are blessed."

That's it and keep moving not looking for a response back because if you don't get one, it may mess up your day.

The Bible says it is easy to love someone who loves you, but harder to love someone who hates you.

Hate is such a widespread word today than ever, people are willing to kill you because you say, "Hello" to them.

I remember I had seen a mother and her teenaged son in a truck and I was trying to find a dental office in the area, so I pulled up beside them and ask directions.

The next thing that took place was I was cursed out and told to go ask someone else they did not have time for that stuff. (other words were used, of course)

That made me think about the people helping me and my ex-wife and how in the end we began to treat each other badly.

Words!

They can make or break a situation. You see, we can't always take the good with the bad if the bad that is coming at you outweighs the good.

Beauty can become ugly.

But God turns ugly into beauty.

Are we getting to the point we are afraid of being alone?

Are we becoming to the point that we feel we are going to die alone?

Is that why we try to do God's work and mess everything up in our lives and wonder why we still die alone anyway?

Have we become a better judge of character in a woman or a man than Jesus?

Have we allowed our mind set to believe that we are just like God?

Who are you?

Who do you think you are?

You did not create anything and you can't even exist without God even if you belong to Satan.

What are you and who do you belong too?

It may hurt.

It may make you feel you are lonely.

It may seem like it will never happen.

You may even start to have doubt. Trust me, I know firsthand.

You want to say yes, but God says no.

You say, "Lord, now?"

He says, "It's not your time yet."

How can that not hurt when others around you are being blessed?

He then says, "I know your pain. Trust in me and all that you have asked for that leads you toward my goals for your life will appear one day and when it does."

Then you will say, "Now I see" and be thankful for the time you had to wait.

God knows waiting on Him comes with a price and that's why he rewards those who wait on him.

The Lord showed me who I could have been and what I would have become had I not change my lifestyle as well as my way of living.

It's all about the choices we make that are pleasing to God.

Not by showing that you are turning your backs on Him.

There are those who follow their own ways who in turn need healing from the outside in and those who follow God's ways and need healing from the inside out.

When you see someone who is following their own way, they may appear sick on the outside. You can tell that something is wrong with them.

It may appear to be some type of disease or element of some kind.

When you are following God and you're in need of healing.

God heals from the inside out. You see the healing is taking place because they are looking like a new person/creature, showing a light of healing through our Lord Jesus.

People are able to see someone free from the bondage of sickness.

Martin Luther King Jr. said it best, "Free at last free at last thank God Almighty we are free at last."

God will appoint and anoint men and women in order to get a message out.

Even if no one is able to see that in the mist of what is going on in our lives.

GOING FROM AN ANGRY MAN TO A PEACEFUL MAN
IS NOT AN EASY JOURNEY

So many people are crying out for help, but we have become so engulfed in our own needs and selfishness that we forgot that there are others that maybe going through more than we are dealing with.

Our children and teens are not laughing anymore, they are crying. The rules have changed and so have the laws.

The Bible talks about the laws of living and the living of faith.

The laws of the world want us to believe their ways are true and wise and that the laws of the Bible are false.

The laws of the world are war and the truth of Jesus is peace and love.

The love of the world has become hate and lust.

Sad to say that it is harder nowadays to even trust the churches of today. Not all are bad, but in today's life there are more that will lead you to Hell then there are that will lead you into Heaven.

Satan will try to destroy what God has created in order to copy the truth with lies.

The biggest lie is that there is nothing after this life so live life like there is no tomorrow.

Take what the world has to offer and worship him and that life is yours forever.

But it only last but for a short while here on earth, but it lasts a lot longer after life in Hell.

In the Bible, it talks about how Satan hates everyone so how can you want what he has to offer knowing this to be a fact?

We obey our Father who is in Heaven and we acknowledge who he is and what he has done.

We also acknowledge that Jesus is our Lord and his name is pleasing to the most high and the great "I Am" Jehovah.

But God said, "Suffer in thy name and give praise and live."

Chose me and chose life. Why is it so hard for people to choose life?

Because it's easier to give up and choose death and gain the world than to fight for life and gain the kingdom.

God also says, "Live not only in this life, but the life after this, but cling not to the things of this world."

Yet people seem not to hear anymore what has been said because now that this is Satan's time to rein it has come true what the Bible talks about to those who have ears hear what the Lord God has to say.

Life is given to those who chose life.

Many will be called, but only a few will choose and be chosen.

The music of today has even changed. It used to be about love and now it's about pain and getting even with someone.

Life used to be about family and now it's about self and what someone can do for me and what I can get from them.

What has happened to the old days?

Are there still people who believe in the ways of love?

Why is it that the children of this time are trying to show us the way but still a lot of people don't care to listen to what they have to say only because they are children?

But the Bible says that out of the mouths of babies follows the word of life.

Is that why the Devil is trying so hard to kill them off?

His children sing of lust and things they want to do to someone and teaching how calling someone out of their name seems to make them want the other person even more.

Nowadays if you call someone by their name, they seem to get mad at you. Call them something else and they love you.

I used to think that being alone was the way to go and as I began to meet people, I found that when you have someone who is a part of your life who is a true friend.

I can understand what the Bible says that man should not be alone.

Not only with friends, but with that one who becomes a part of your life until God calls you both home.

At one time, I used to think that being alone was okay, no one to trouble you or tell you what to do.

But that was all a lie, you have no one to talk with or to do things with.

So many people are starting to believe that being alone is okay and they find themselves dying alone with no one to grieve over them in their time of death because no one knew they lived.

No one knew they lived what a way to go.

Hmmmm.

You find yourself sitting and crying alone with no one to comfort you, even when you are sick looking around and no one's there.

You begin to live in pain from being alone with no help or no one around you to reach out too.

No one to hold your hand and say it will all be alright.

Look up to the Heavens right now and ask Jesus to free you from that feeling of wanting to be alone and of feeling content with it right now.

Not saying you will go through a spell in your life when you will be alone, but don't try to fix it on your own. Again, pray to God for the one who should and will be in your life.

True!

We have all been hurt before and have lost someone in our lives that has caused us to want to close ourselves away from the world and not want to belong anymore.

But do stand and fight or give up and let your soul die and fad away along with your life?

Why are so many people starting to run from the Lord? Please turn your lives around and run back to him.

Don't become lost and not able to find your way back to Him.

He is waiting and wanting you to come back to him, his one little lost lamb out of one hundred and now down to ninety-nine.

The Bible says that you're the one the shepherd will leave his flock to bring back home.

I don't believe it to be true and that is it's fun being alone.

It's not fun at all.

But I have come to find that even if you are with someone, it does not mean you're not alone.

I have a question.

I want to ask and I really need for you to think of the question before you answer.

The question is: Are you happy with being by yourself and alone?

The next question is: Can you be happy by yourself and alone?

But you see the questions don't stop there, they only begin.

Let's start with the people in your life. Do they make you feel alone, seen but not heard?

Sometimes heard but not seen?

Let me explain what I mean.

Have you ever sat in a room with one person or a group of people everyone is talking about things that have taken place in their lives?

You know the group of people have been friends for some time and now you have come into the group as a new friend.

As they are talking and you begin to tell your story, it seems as though no one really wants to hear what you have to say because you are the stranger looking in at them.

So every time you say something, you begin to notice someone else would try to change the subject or for some reason the story you were telling did not interest the group because it was coming from you.

What you had to share did not deal with the group; it did not have anything to do with the things they have done together or were talking about.

Leaving you feeling alone and unwanted.

Has your spouse or the person you are dealing with ever made you feel that way?

Have you ever been in a room of people and they ask why are you so quiet and you begin to speak and then you're not seen? They stop seeing that you are there and begin talking about themselves again?

What happened to being able to talk with someone about how you feel without them trying to make it seem like you have the problem?

Only because they only hear and see what they want and that is themselves. You and your feelings are not important, it's only about their lives.

There are so many with wounded hearts in the world today, but no one hears them anymore. People are starting to stop caring.

All we want to do is fuss and fight and say its love.

This is what they call love.

If we can see what is going on, then we can pray to Jesus for help in order to make a change from the negative direction we are on to getting use on point in order to begin a positive road to walk down.

When you feel like you're doing something wrong, do you not want to try to find a way to make it right?

Well, most people in this time and age of life know they are doing wrong things, yet they don't want change.

They are happy doing wrong it brings them joy doing wrong.

Do we understand what true friendship is today?

Is it, "I am your friend until what you have that I want runs out and then we can't be friends anymore"?

The kiss good-bye.

This is some people, but then you have those who just drive people away and the funny thing is they don't even know that they do this.

Ask yourself, do you understand what a true friendship is and it's not just having someone around when they need you?

Are they around when you're in need of them or are they to busy when it comes to you?

But it happens the other way around as well.

You're too busy when you don't have a need for them.

Have you ever thought being in charge of someone or in control of someone made you feel like you were better than them?

Why would one want to give up on a gift from God for a life of unhappiness?

Who you are inside will come out sooner or later.

Not a lot of people value the life that Jesus died and gave for us that we are still able to be living and given a chance to pick life or death.

Some of the things we get for free has a greater price on it then we can ever understand or realize.

There are groups of people who pull you into their lifestyle by promises of worldly gifts and trophies.

JAMES E. MCCULLOUGH

When you sign on the dotted line with these groups, you sign your life away as they did at one time.

How do you feel about a gift that is only death?

The trophy is you walking around showing how you chose death over life and how proud you are.

You get a call and someone on the other end says your dying, I chose to give you death because you wanted it so badly.

You were willing to sell your soul for it and signed on the dotted line without reading the contract.

You should have at least read it once instead because of what was offered you decided to receive something you cannot exchange. There are no exchanges, all sales are final.

We can talk about these situations with sex, joining gangs, murder, anything that one knows is wrong.

It's easy to gain the negative things in life, but harder to live with the price you'll have to pay for it.

Just like we guys sit around talking about the women, we have concord last week even yesterday.

But not something such as I meet this woman and we got together and now I have something I can't return.

This is both ways men and women.

Some people are like this, "If you ask me, I don't have to tell you the truth."

You really don't want to ask the person you are with if they are safe.

You really don't care anyway. What you want is right know. You'll worry about tomorrow but at this moment this is what we are sharing right now.

Each other.

Or when a gang member asks his brother or sister to join their gang, but first you have to prove yourself for example killing another family member.

Someone you don't know, an old lady or old man.

Some pregnant woman coming from a doctor's appointment or the person who you come into contact with that has a certain color.

But the whole thing is there is no real reason behind this act.

Take a life in order to save your own, until your life is taken and now your life exists behind bars without the possibility of ever having freedom in this life and it could also go into the next life as well.

So many people ask the question: How can you get mad and hurt or kill someone?

Anger is like a bullet it has no name or face on it, it's just something that appears without notice in one's spirit.

When it is setting in you and it is released, you are not yourself but something else.

The Bible says to be slow to anger.

When you become angry, you release a demand inside you that you cannot control.

That's why you should and need to call on Jesus and just the name of Jesus.

Jesus himself, the name is real and strong; Jesus, Jesus, Jesus I need you Jesus right now right here. Please Jesus, without your help I surely will die.

I am in need of you to fight these demands that are trying to obtain my life, my soul.

Heavenly Father, if you don't intervene on my behalf, I will surely die.

I can't and I don't want to live someone else's life. It's hard enough living my own.

How far are you willing to go in order to get ahead, who are you willing to hurt, use or try to destroy in order to build a business or to make money.

To prove to someone, you've got what it takes to get what you want at no cost.

There is this by no means necessary attitude.

People forget that all you do comes back in ways later in life yet we still ask this question "Lord why me."

All the things done in our past comes back at some point.

Did you make a family member or friend feel like you were stronger to them inside because you felt like they had no voice and what they had to say didn't matter only because you were in charge?

You felt like you didn't have to listen to what they had to say because it was your way or no way at all.

This being said to you because they see how you have changed, but you have those who see no wrong in anything you do.

Have you ever had someone ask you for advice only to say in your face can anyone else help me, because what you had to say seems wrong because it does not line up with what they want to hear?

The truth!

They are only willing and wanting to hear the lie which says all is well when all is not.

In 1 Corinthians 10: 13 it says, "No temptation has overtaken you except such as is common to man; but God is faithful, who will not allow you to be tempted beyond what you are able, but with the temptation will also make the way of escape, that you may be able to bear it."

Let me ask this of you, are you happy with yourself?

Do people around you ask others why you're alone or why they never see you with someone else?

Does that make you want to go out and prove them wrong?

Do you feel that you can't make it on your own or by yourself being alone?

The person or people you surround yourself with, are you able to be yourself around them or are they your controller?

People have a way of taking control over your life without you even being aware of it taking place.

Have you ever had someone tell you that your going to have something wonderful happen in your life?

So, at once your mind takes a mental picture of what was said to you and this is how things get started.

You begin to see this thing taking place and you believe it to happen.

Let's say that you are married and someone tells you that you will meet someone who will sweep you off your feet.

So, you begin working on this happening in your life only you forget that you have a spouse.

Or let's say that you have a gift and someone you meet sees that gift so they say, "I have to find the right words to say to them in order to take control of this person, but I have to make them think it was their own idea."

You see, in any situation I have learned that when you talk to someone about your problems, they may take what you talked to them about and use it against you so that it benefits them.

When you complain about something going wrong, they tell you how they can make it right.

Making you believe that it's you saying how you can change what's going on in your life.

But they have become the puppeteer and you the puppet but your ears have been closed to the ways of God and open to Satan.

You begin to tell them what was said or done to you and that's always the best time to strike when they/you can't see what's going to happen because of what was said to the outside source the defiling stranger.

Jesus was rightly concerned with the heart Saying.

It is not what goes into the mouth that defiles a person, but what comes out of the mouth; this defiles a person.

Matthew 15:11 – "What comes out of the mouth proceeds from the heart, and this defiles a person."

Matthew 15:18 – "And not what goes into the mouth. What is it that Jesus was referring when He said "but what comes out of the mouth that defiles a person?"

It was the words we use because our words reveal what is in our heart and if we are defiled before God it is because our words betray us for out of our mouth speaks the hidden in the heart.

The devil begins to say, "I am about to ruin what you are used to. I will turn your entire world around. But first you have to follow me your life will not remain the same, I want to bring you into my world."

Have you ever told someone that I hate you?

Did you know why you said those words?

Do you understand why you were not affected emotionally?

Even though you knew you were hurting the one you said these things too.

You're spouse a friend, your son or daughter, your mother or father?

Jesus!

To this very day you still have no remorse towards what you said.

But please don't forget your actions that went along with those words.

Doing wrong causes destruction.

There is so much crime in the world, yet when something horrific happens to an individual or in another country.

We as a people speak of peace.

But only for a moment and then we go back to who we were before these things took place.

Self, no one else is important someone may have lost their life, but yet you don't care anymore.

How someone who was out sleeping around and caught HSV 1 & 2 or how someone has HIV or died of AIDS.

People still don't stop.

The worst part about this is most of these same people say, "Since it happened to me, I have to do the same thing to someone else."

How far are you willing to go in order to get your way or climb to the top?

How many people are you willing to hurt?

Before you realize your only headed to the bottom?

The reason I ask this question is because the devil says, "You have to follow me first but you don't have to give up anything but the God you serve."

This is what the people who are in your life ask of you as well.

But first you have to give up something in order to receive what I have to offer to you.

Sometimes you give up something that you can never get back.

Not a person or a thing but yourself.

Your soul.

I remember after writing the first book *Understanding the Power of God* I gave a year to which I would finish book number two.

But not realizing God had other plans on the date in which book number two would be coming out.

You see, even we as humans feel like if things don't happen when we want them to.

Well we have to take matters into our own hands.

But because of us going to others outside of a marriage or relationship and even friendship talking to the Devil in a negative way.

We forget that we are not perfect and that love brings pain and praying to God heals.

Most people when you go to them with negative talk about someone.

They never ask what part of this is your fault.

Is there a reason why all this is happening?

Other than just accepting what one person has to say, sit and talk to them both in order to get both sides.

Most people open their minds and hearts to one who knows how to play the victim.

But they close their heart and mind to the situation. What is the real truth?

Everything doesn't come from one person.

I remember Jesus saying to me, "How can I have you write about a journey that you have not been on becoming a man who goes from anger to peace?"

The thing is, the man made of flesh is still there seeking the spirit of peace within himself.

Only once you have gone on the journey can peace be found.

One thing I had to learn was the meaning of the word "help".

Help is not a hand out but what you work towards. It's there to educate you on what you need to learn on the ways to please God through your growth and understanding.

Jesus is teaching us not to look for a handout, but how to work for what we are in need of faith because faith without works is dead.

Jesus is educating us on the ways of learning how to please the Father because through Him is where your help comes from.

Through growth and understanding while you are going through your trials and walk through the wilderness will determine how you come out in the end.

Will you become a man of peace or will the anger continue to overtake you?

From whom does your help come from?

I know for a lot of you having the feeling that you heart had been ripe out now days are becoming very common.

The thing is how you deal with the broken heart syndrome because everyone deals with this matter in a different way.

This is a question a lot of people ask within themselves.

How can you be a part of something you have no part of belonging to?

Is our house a house that belongs to us as a whole or is it your house?

I am not even a guest who is supposed to feel welcomed there?

Have you ever been made to feel that way at home as well as the church you belong to?

Have you ever got yourself ready for church on Saturday night for church Sunday morning?

You thought that you were prayed up for yourself and for all of the members of the church, but as you slept through the night you had a nightmare of what was going to take place the next morning.

Yet you still get up and begin once more to praise the Lord and get ready and right from the start you are attacked by the enemy and you want to leave right then and there, but you stay.

Only because it's not about you, but about what God is saying as well as showing you.

Sometimes God will test your strength to see if you will stand or if you will flee.

In 1 Peter 1: 3-5 it says, "Blessed be the God and Father of our Lord Jesus Christ, who according to His abundant mercy has begotten us again to a living hope through the resurrection of Jesus Christ from the dead, to an inheritance incorruptible and undefiled and that does not fade away, reserved in Heaven for you, who are kept by the power of God through faith for salvation ready to be revealed in the last time."

The strength we stand on is not our own, it is the Lord's.

People make talk about you and even put you down when they are not in front of you.

In John 10: 27-29 it says, "My sheep hear My voice, and I know them, and they follow Me. And I give them eternal life, and they shall never perish; neither shall anyone snatch them out of My hand. My Father, who has given them to Me, is greater than all; and no one is able to snatch them out of My Father's hand."

So you see in the word of the Lord He says even when we are not there to defend ourselves, He is there to defend us.

Trust in God because man will always let you down, but Jesus is always in the mist of all things good and bad that takes place in our lives.

So many people are turning away from church as they are dropping out of school nowadays.

Churches are closing just as fast as schools, but with both it affects those that are willing and wanting to learn.

God's word at one time was in the schools for the children that want to learn.

There are so many false prophets and men and women of God, people are running from the church, but there running to talk show host and radio show host for answers.

What happened to praying to God?

You can't trust the men and women of the church nowadays because they use what you say against you in these days, most are only out for self-gain.

The trust factor is now out of style and drama has taken its place.

Someone said, "If you talk to someone about the person you're dealing with in a negative way, what makes you think that they aren't talking about you in the same manner?"

When someone makes you feel you don't belong, does it make you want to stay?

Have you ever had a long day at work and felt like when you got home all would be made easier?

You say to the people you work with, "I am on my way home and I have someone waiting for me and when I open that door and walk in all the stress of the world will just fall right off my body."

You are on your way home setting your spirit to be in the right mood.

You pull up to the house.

You get out of the car and go up to the door and put the key in the lock and turn the key.

But instead of feeling welcomed, you felt like you wanted to turn around and leave and say to yourself, "I must have walked through the wrong door or went to the wrong house."

What happened to making the person feel welcomed in the house you both share?

We can make each other feel unwelcome because it's not our home but the other persons.

We can make our spouse feel like if they say or do something we don't like because we are in control we have to make them feel bad, but if I do the same things as you because it's my house it's no problem.

It doesn't matter if one so called had the house first you made a decision to live together as one.

Or if it is a house of a ready-made family, they all treat you like you are nothing, having no respect for you and when you're not around, talk about you.

These are things that make you want to say this is your last kiss good bye.

There are times we chase after a storm someone who doesn't want to be caught so they tell you that this is the last kiss good-bye.

Yet they still want you to chase after them, but how can one catch the wind?

How do you catch a storm when it will swallow you up and spit you out maybe even kill you in the end?

If you have never been caught in a storm, the winds are so strong that they blow you or push you away with great force.

Some people get caught in that force and it leads to their death.

God will tell us a lot of the times to let go and stop chasing the wind and seek his face, because He closed one door in order to opened a new.

One kiss good-bye could be another kiss HELLO.

God says in Matthew 19:29, "And everyone who has left houses or brothers or sisters or father or mother or wife or children or lands, for my name's sake, shall receive a hundredfold, and inherit eternal life."

There are people that just don't belong together and it's no one person's fault. That's what makes us different and what makes us who we are.

There are so many people in the world, but don't give up on knowing that one of them is for you and that one day Jesus will bring you into the others presence.

What normally brings us down is the way that we treat each other now days.

I want to speak from things that I myself experience and it breaks my heart at times because life has not always been this way.

I am a black male and I love my black woman, but they tend to look at most black men as if they are dirt without knowing anything about them.

They know not who they are or who's they are, but then again maybe they do in spirit and as the Bible says, "good and evil cannot live together".

So, I want us all to understand.

When you see someone and you smile at them and even say, "Hello."

They may look at you from head to toe and then look down at the ground and say nothing to you.

That's because you are not the same as they are.

People tend to migrate with people who are like them.

So don't be offended.

The children of God migrate towards each other and so does the children of Satan.

Some who read this maybe mad, but it's true even the fake people who say they are for God but are too good to give someone a smile or even a kind Hello.

Most people are not looking for love there looking for lust.

Are you seeking the face of love and long suffering which is Jesus or are you seeking the face of lust and everything being given to you now the world's way of thinking?

You may not be suffering now but getting everything you want without caring for no one, then you seek the face of Satan.

"Who do you serve?" is a true question.

You need to seek the truth within yourself because you may be serving the wrong God.

There is only one God and one Lord and Savior that lives and gives life and who has given his life that we may live after this life is over.

Let's look at Eternal Life: life everlasting represents man's final victory over sin and death.

Revelations 21:4 In the New Living Translation; He will remove all of their sorrows, and there will be no more death or sorrow or crying or pain. For the old world and its evils are gone forever.

So let's look at giving a kiss or embrace and saying "Hello" instead of the last kiss good-bye.

Chapter 6

Prayer and tears; God will you forgive me? Father God I also ask for direction

When I first began writing this, I wasn't sure of how I wanted to begin.

I knew my life was going in the wrong direction and I knew it had to change.

This is real life lessons we all need to learn.

When will you see the need to change yourself?

At first, I was going to share with you some different information.

Some people look at life as a comedy.

Either their life or someone else's.

It appears to them like it's a comedy sense.

When are you going to stop living your life as the joker while people are laughing at you behind your back?

They begin to make you feel like a fool in front of your face.

What direction are you trying to go?

At first, I was going to tell you a different story, but this story would not be a comedy but a real true-life story that had me not knowing who I was.

There are so many people who may be able to relate to this.

Tragedy seems to fuel the fire of someone who finds a person who they feel has nowhere to turn, but control and desire ignite the fire to try to rule one's life, but if you look towards the Heavens and call on this name.

Jesus!

Jesus, he will set you free as he did me in this story you are about to read.

Growing up for me was not easy at all. Trying to find a job, I left Pittsburgh and I had good jobs, but I didn't know how to manage my money.

No one to guide me because I didn't know Jesus.

But when I got to know him, I still made the same mistakes.

I had a job working as a security guard, most of the areas I worked.

Now for some reason the landscape appeared to look like the seats in a church.

It seemed as though the side walk was a stage.

When I first started going to church, I could see myself as a pastor.

So, as I looked around the spirit of the Holy Ghost came over me.

I looked out and I felt like I needed to pray to people in the spirit, even myself.

I then began to sing songs that were given to me and I started teaching in the spirit.

I would see different things in the spirit as I thought the word of God that was coming out of me in to the spirit world.

I would see the land scape and it looked as though it was an arena filled with people.

So, I would walk up and down like as if I was on the pulpit preaching to people in the aisles.

I would teach and sing.

It seemed like most of the areas that I worked in would take me back to a church arena setting.

So every time I was placed in that type of setting, I would sing and teach into the different types of land scapings.

I began to change and I had no idea why.

So one day I said, "Heavenly Father, who am I?"

I feel so different inside. I have been trying to do good and it seems like the harder I try the more I'm under attack, but I won't give up I will not stop praying, trusting or believing in you.

I'm afraid to stop having hope in you, because if I stop, I am afraid I'll die.

I'm afraid of death, but I am not afraid of dying.

When I'm dead, my body can't live again and if my work for you Jesus is not done, have I given up the chance at being able to live in God's kingdom?

Will I only be able to look up saying as I look toward the Heavens, "Father God, can I have another chance?"

Only because I rejected you while I was still alive.

Because I lived a life of continued sin never looking back and never repenting or asking for forgiveness.

But then I was told when I die there is a chance for life after death not of the body but of the spirit.

In Ecclesiastes 12:7, "And the dust returns to the earth as it was, and the spirit returns to God who gave it."

When we pray while living asking God to forgive us of our sins and repenting of our sins as we look up toward the Heavens and ask Jesus for another chance, he hears your cries.

The reason being is because I hope I get into Heaven and because I tried to live my life right.

Yes, I mess up at times probably, more than one, but not to say that I don't try to live my life according to the will of our Heavenly Father.

Seeking His direction for my life.

These are the questions that I had been asking and that of our Heavenly Father to give me guidance and to give me direction.

Also to let me know who I am.

How many of you can say that Jesus had shown you or spoke with you about something and it has happened or it has not happened yet?

How does it make you feel if it has not happened as of yet?

How does your heart and your spirit feel right now?

How do you feel about Jesus?

How do you feel about your life?

For those of you who have receive the blessing in your life has it changed you in anyway?

Do you still believe and serve the one who blessed you with it?

Is it the things we get or don't get that makes us love or lose faith in the true God of life?

Chapter 7

When you stop caring for Jesus and His Children

Heavenly Father, what am I doing wrong? It seems like everything I touch fades away instead of turning to gold.

Most of the jobs I've had here lately I've been taken advantage of and mistreated.

It seems that has become the new way of life now.

It seems when I move ahead, I am brought back down once more.

It seems to be harder and harder to get back up.

Closer and closer to almost losing everything once more.

I work and I look at some of the things other people have and I ask myself, "What are they doing that I'm not? Why is it that I'm working so hard to have and it seems like they are not working at all and yet they have so much? Lord what am I doing wrong?"

Lord, I know that all things gained are not always good for us, so no matter how my life may seem now I know that you are able to bless me here on earth or when I get to Heaven.

I must keep joy in my heart and singing is my spirit because only if I receive my blessings from you can I enjoy them.

People may say, "Well, you have been struggling all your life."

But the struggle was to be like someone else and to please someone else.

I didn't know how to be me I became jealous of everyone around me.

They say that money is the root of all evil, yet so many people are reaching out for money in so many different ways.

For a lot of people, you I have to ask what happened "to seek ye first the kingdom of God and all things will be added to you"?

He did not say that all things would be good or that you would get all that you ask for.

He did say that all your needs he would supply and that he would not put more on you then you can handle.

What has happened to the men and the women of God is that the money they have is not making them happy it's nice to have it in your life.

So now it seems as though so many people are now living their lives.

Yet now they have forgotten the days when God's work was important.

They have stopped looking out for God's children.

Now you have to understand people are helping people all over the world yet the children we see every day are dying on the street.

Every now and then you hear about someone being a blessing to someone.

What has happened in your life that you are doing so much living for yourself and have so much fun in your life that you forgot about the struggle before God blessed you.

Not all, but so many are living their lives.

Yet not dying for Jesus anymore.

Living for the fulfillment of self and flesh.

Yet now they preach on how someone else should live or be.

People are being ran away from churches because of how they are being treated by leaders and some members.

A lot of people reading this may be getting mad right about now.

But it's the truth sometimes the people of God treat you worst then the people of the world.

You have so many people who are now starting their own churches because they see that it's big money in it today.

GOING FROM AN ANGRY MAN TO A PEACEFUL MAN
IS NOT AN EASY JOURNEY

Your looking at this right.

They say I can start a church for making money because money is now becoming a lot of peoples God.

Pastors are wanting what other pastors have and some have become hard and cold to members in the church that God set them up with in order to lead and to feed his children.

But when it comes to helping someone in need it has become so hard to get help from the church.

Jobs are just as hard to find even in the church now not everyone was able to finish high school.

I remember when the church would help for free.

They worked with different organizations that would help people to get jobs.

It seems as if all of a sudden in order to get a job you have to go through a temp agency and you may or may not get the job.

It's not as easy anymore to get a real job that pays what you are worth just what they want you to have.

Most of the time they have no respect for the people through the temp agencies.

So many people are starting to feel unappreciated.

Yet they still believe in Jesus and believe in his word because he still provides all their needs.

You have a lot of celebrities who give and do for people to be seen for what they are doing.

I understand you have to be in the light with what you do, it's important to you that people see you as someone with a heart or should we say the public.

There are people with so much money they will never run out of it.

When you do for a charity, does it always have to be the same one all the time?

It's getting now so that if you don't have a college degree no one in the church can help you find a job let alone give you a job.

A lot of celebrities have companies and businesses as do churches.

Can anyone step up more with helping people without diplomas get a or be given a job that's not in a sweat shop and can't live on the money they are being given?

It's said when you work so hard and still can't pay your bills and eat at the same time.

Something is wrong.

There are real people trying and I'm one of them that sit back and watch the ones who get opportunities waste it once they get it and mess things up for the next person.

If they do give you a job it's making minimum wage and you're working harder than anyone else because they know you're in need and to them you're not a person.

You have now become someone who is only good until they run out of things they need done.

The quicker you get done, the sooner they don't need you anymore.

It's to the point most companies and people have no feelings for human life.

You have become a thing, not a person.

Don't get sick or hurt nothing that would cause you to stop making money for them, because they will get mad at you.

If you get hurt now, they have to pay money out and you have now cost them a lose you are no longer a money maker to them.

Have you or do you work for a company that makes you work six days a week maybe even seven.

Sometimes over twelve or fifteen hours a day and if you say something about it, they tell you that if you don't like it, they can hire someone who is willing to work the hours.

Now most people have families and a life, but now your life belongs to the job.

You tell them you go to church on Sundays so now that is one of the days you are assigned to work.

You tell them about your family and your time is taken so that you don't have time to spend with them.

Your body begins to show signs of early aging, yet you don't see it or know it until someone tells you.

Has anyone ever walked up to you and said do you get enough sleep you have big dark spots around your eyes?

On your days off do you do more sleeping than anything else?

Do you work over one hundred hours in one week just to make a decent pay check?

Only because you only make eight to nine dollars and hour but these long hours don't seem that much because of the money your making.

The money your making with your health and your life span is getting shorter each day.

God said I will make your life long, not shorter.

But the mind game that has been played on you the people has now been turned around money has become your God.

Your family has to now take the loss of not being able to spend time with you as much if at all.

The thing is we say it will only be for a little while.

The things of the world today have taken away the balance of happiness and prosperity.

It has turned to greed, lust, and coldness of heart.

Has your heart ever become hardened with the more money you made?

Do you know someone who's heart became hardened with the more money they made?

There are people who are being blessed with wealth and then there are others who are becoming cursed.

There is a question you need to ask yourself: In what category do I fit in and in which direction am I headed?

You see to find out to late that you are headed in the direction of being cursed and not know it has a price to pay in this life or the afterlife.

When greed steps in and the value of a human life becomes less important to you and all you see is if someone can't or won't make you money then they have and are of no value to you.

When someone gets sick or hurt on a job and even if they can still preform their jobs because they were not there when you felt they should have been you dismiss or let them go.

To order or allow to leave; send away.

Yet when you were struggling and praying to God asking him to give you a way out and how you would help others.

Which God as they say where you praying and making such a flash confession too.

It was not the true God of Heaven but the God that has been given dominion over the earth.

God of Heaven gives you a heart that is alive not dead.

Why is it that one starts off with a good heart, then when you see how money can change your life it changes you spirit?

Money can buy you all kinds of things, but it can't buy you a place into Heaven.

So many disbelieve that this is true.

People say I can buy my way into Heaven or that they are richer than God himself.

How can one say something like that?

No one is God but God.

He does not compete with us all things belong to him even that which you think you received on your own.

Fear the Lord.

His wrath is true and so is his word and the things He has promised to those who would want to gain the world.

Why do you think God says he has his children and Satan has his?

Heaven and Hell are two different places and neither is here on earth.

Why do you think no one has been able to see beyond the true skies Heaven and no one has ever been able to see the true center of the earth Hell?

They are two spirit realms that no one alive will see they will begiven a glimpse, but to be shown the true state of Heaven or Hell would be standing in front of the sun with nothing to protect you.

It would destroy you.

Jesus only allows to see what you are able to see and live to tell that which he needs the world to know.

But you need to know that Satan does the same in order to fool the fool.

These are some of the things that make people of all ages get made about in life.

How can we come together and make an affective change?

The way it stands now the devil is here to destroy the family.

To take away your joy and still your hope and life.

To get you to stop believing in the one true living God and our Lord Jesus.

People have stopped believing that Jesus is our Savior.

On March 3 2019, after going to Bible study and then to church service, God said to me because of what was said in Bible study.

Acceptance dealing with what I was going through was what I needed prayer for dealing with what was going on in my life.

But then Jesus said when we except the things that are going on in our lives that are bad then we shut down the opportunity for change.

Jesus spoke to me during the 6:00 pm service he said the need for change and blessing only. comes when you walk away from people, places, and objects.

The vices we feel we need to sustain us that we have not been able to see the damage that is being done in our lives.

How many times have you walk away from me to interact with the vices you ran to instead of running to me?

I bless you and you walk away from me.

Now will you walk with me and continue to walk with me and not stray from me anymore that I may bless you with that which I have been wanting to give you.

Which my heart has been longing to give you.

Your eye's have been shut from the things you've had to go through.

The hurts the pain and sacrifices I seen you make.

When I know your heart is truly mine, I will give you that which will allow you to know who I am.

My child no my son or daughter.

When we look back in our history.

What was that change in your life that made it impossible or hindered you to be able to go forward instead of being stuck in the same place?

That is the question we all need to ask ourselves.

What happened to the passion?

What was so strong and that took control over your emotions and your life that took you to another place that lead you away from your walk with Jesus?

How can we stop walking around pretending that our lives are okay when we know that what we feel and what is taking place in our lives are not the same?

Sometimes when I talk to people; I just want to say will you please stop talking and listen to what I am saying!

Please listen.

You see we all want to talk but we don't hear what the other person is saying because we think we know what they are feeling inside.

People run from God because people don't listen.

Leaders of the church listen.

We have stopped listening because we have become so spiritual that we have forgot how to listen in the time of someone's needs.

Sometimes you have to ask yourself this question am I leading people to Jesus or am I driving them away because I have not listened to what they had to say?

But instead I said what made me feel like I understood, when in reality I never heard a word that was said.

I'm not just writing just because, but because this seems to happen to me time and time again.

It makes one want to say I don't want to talk about me when you feel you already know all about my life without even knowing or hearing what I have to say.

What if it was your son or daughter your husband or your wife you father or mother would you listen.

What if it was you would you want someone to listen and not speak for you?

Chapter 8

In today's world searching for love is not an easy journey

Did you know that when God takes you through different trails in life as well as the paths that one walks through in the wilderness, it's not for you to come out of it being able to receive blessing, meaning you will get the desires of your heart according to His will.

Jesus allows you to go through it in order for you to get and understanding of life.

This is done in order that you understand who you belong too.

You need to understand the meaning of life according to the God you follow.

The reason being is because God the Heavenly Father which is in Heaven not in the earth is life and the one and only true God.

If you can't understand that stop!

This is a true question; I need you to think where He is in your life and where you are is His.

Do you understand who Jesus is and what He gave for you?

Do you understand that in order to reach the Heavenly Father Jehovah that you must go through Jesus Christ?

If God were to put this question to you how would you respond: Who's life style do you want to continue to live mine or yours.

What if Jesus said to you that the choice you make right now will change your life.

What would your answer be?

He then shared this with me (a wise man does not see wisdom; it's shown when he speaks to others as well as how he treats them.

Only then can they see Jesus and God will reveal himself through each person who has become one of his own).

Love was once like a beautiful poem something like this one.

Love is like the wind on a cool Summers night.

All is still except the movement and sounds of two hearts beating as one.

Thump goes one thump goes the second.

The hearts begin to go thump, thump, thump in motion together.

As love grows it's like the cycle of seasons, winter, spring, summer and fall seeing how each one waits patiently for their time to come not rushing or getting up-set with each other no matter how long it takes for their season to begin.

Because sometimes the seasons seem to go over with their time and some seasons seem to be shorter, but if we truly understand love no matter who seems to be blessed if you are in Jesus and he in you then love continues to bet through each one of you as one heart bet thump, thump.

Because when God blesses one of you; are you not blessed together being that you are one.

God the Father, Jesus the son and the Holy Spirit all work as one.

They don't work against each other because they are one in the same.

That's how you should see love in your lives.

When Jesus died for you and me.

What if he would have said.

Father I am giving up more than they know.

I will go through more pain then they can every imagine.

Father you and I already know that they will never appreciate what you are asking of me to do for them.

You see then he would have been like me and you.

Jesus was not selfish nor was he a man of only flesh and blood he was the true spirit that now lives in us all.

He set us free from death.

Yet we continue to refuse life and we are willing to choose and except death.

Why then are we doing this?

What if Jesus said why should I give my life for these people who are ungrateful?

But you see none of these questions or in some cases none of this anger was felt.

No one through up in each other's faces who was doing more or giving up more.

It was all done because of the love in the Father the Son being Jesus and the Holy Spirit.

Even though people looked at Jesus as an animal that they bet and had no feelings for him as far as him being human at the time, not knowing that the spirit in him was the spirit whose heart was not of this earth.

The heart that bled here on earth was the blood of Heaven if Jesus was not sacrificed God could not heal the land and the people through the blood of Jesus nor could he allow us to live.

What are you willing to sacrifice for that kind of love?

I did not say who are you willing to sacrifice.

I said what of yourself are you willing to sacrifice according to your ways and your life style.

Love!!!

Remember God loves us so much that he offered his only son that he would come to earth in the form of flesh.

Because he looked at us humans as one of importance, we've gotten to become so far from that.

It has become a world of I have to become number one and no one else matters even if you are hurting someone else because someone is hurting you.

Seek love before it's too late.

You know that Heaven and Hell are real and you may not understand the chose you make now could change the course of your life.

You do have a chose.

So many people say I'm going to live my life like there is no tomorrow, but there may not be a tomorrow here on earth but there is after death.

We read the Bible but do we ask God to show us how to live love and not go through the motions of love.

I want to understand how to live love each and every day.

So, I ask Jesus how do I feel love in order to understand how to live love each and every day in order to be like you.

He then said to me in order for the process of healing to begin answer this question for me when and why also what made you stop loving yourself in return you stopped loving me?

Love can never be found unless it's lost.

Blind lost can't lead one to love.

That is because if you are blind to not seeing that love does not exist in your life how can you lead others.

When you lose love and seek Jesus in order to find it, he then reveals to you the actions needed to take place in order to find it with in yourself first.

The healing will always start within you before you can show or lead others to find it with in themselves.

Stop allowing the blind to lead you and allow the creator of love to teach you.

When will you Start?

Healing from Past Hurts, Poor Choices and Wrong Decision.

Let's start with Decisions what does the word Decision mean?

Decision Means: A form of judgment.

A conclusion or resolution reached after consideration.

To put it another way I'll do it on my own.

We face decisions every day, how can we determine the best choices to make, especially in the big decisions and the ones that seemingly have no clear answer?

(Genesis: 13:5-15) Abram (later called Abraham) and Lot and the decision to work or not work together.

In the Bible God talks about fighting our battles, God could have stopped the crucifixion of Jesus at any time.

Do you think that God wanted to see His son Jesus become a victim of a slow and painful execution?

Jesus could have gotten mad and said I am getting down from here right now, I can't believe I am putting myself through all this for these people and they could really care less who I am or what I'm giving up for them.

What if God said to Jesus; son I will not let you go through this crucifixion why should I love these people who don't love me or care for me?

If that had taken place then Satan would be God.

We need to realize that the God we serve is Love, Jesus is Love and when you allow the Holy spirit into your life you become love, but you must allow the Father the Son and the Holy Spirit in at the same time because as they say, they come as a package.

I thank God that he is a true God one who when he says he will do something he does it.

One who says what he is going to do and makes it happen, because one is not forced to do His will, but will do it willingly and freely.

God fights your battles because we can't see what or enemies are doing, just like in the movie "The Passion of Christ" you saw how Satan moved around plotting and scheming.

The word scheming: given to or involved in making secret underhanded plans, to make plans, especially in a devious way or with intent to do something illegal or wrong.

We cannot see when these things are being done to us.

So, are you willing to live your life with no covering?

Or are you willing to just let anyone fight your battles?

When our Heavenly Father is willing to fight them for you.

This way you are able to have total victory over your enemies, not saying that it will be with no pain and you would not have some suffering along the way.

Jesus did it for you are you will to do it for Him, the decision is yours to make.

Now let's talk about Choices. What does the word choice mean?

Choice Means: The right, power, or opportunity to choose, option.

An act or instance of choosing, selection.

Free Will: Probably the most common definition of free will is the "ability to make choices without any prior prejudice, inclination, or disposition," and specifically that these "free will" choices are not ultimately predestined by God.

According to the Bible, however, the choices of man are not only ultimately determined by God, but morally determined by one's nature.

Man is indeed a free moral agent and freely makes choices, but in his natural state he necessarily acts in accordance with his fallen nature.

Man willingly makes choices that flow from the heart, and sin is also always attributed to the desires of the heart (James 1:13-15).

When a person turns to Christ, he does so not of his own "free will", but because God has supernaturally enabled and moved him to do so through regeneration.

God never coerces man's will, rather God gives the ability to believe through the work of the Holy Spirit.

This is a doctrinal distinction between the theologies of Calvinism and Arminianism: In Arminianism, God saves those who believe of their own free will.

In Calvinism, God saves those who willingly believe as a result of sovereign enablement by the regenerating work of the Spirit.

Rather than man's will being free, Jesus tells us that, "everyone who commits sin is a slave to sin, "(John 8:34). The heart, until born again, is "deceitful above all things, and desperately sick. (Jeremiah 17:9). God saw in man "every intention of the thoughts of his heart was only evil continually".

(Genesis 6:5). "No one can come to me unless the Father who sent me draws him. And I will raise him up on the last day".

(John 6:44). Man is most free in Heaven, where he is morally unable to sin. True freedom isn't freedom to sin, but freedom from sin.

Now Let's Talk About Hurt. What Does the Word Hurt Mean?

Cause physical pain or injury to: Injure, wound, damage, abuse, disable, incapacitate, maim, mutilate, wrench.

(Ephesians 4:29-32). Let no unwholesome word proceed from your mouth, but only such a word as is good for edification according to the need of the moment, that it may give grace to those who hear.

And do not grieve the Holy Spirit of God, by whom you were sealed for the day of redemption.

Let all bitterness and wrath and anger and clamor and slander be put away from you, along with all malice.

And be kind to one another, tender- hearted, forgiving each other, just as God in Christ also has forgiven you.

Let's talk about the word Healing. What Does the Word Healing Mean?

Rapha To Heal. The process of making or becoming sound or healthy again.

Lessen the gravity of (an offense or mistake).

The word translated "healed "can mean either spiritual or physical.

However, if you look at the contexts of Isaiah 53 and 1 Peter 2 makes it clear that it is speaking of spiritual healing.

"He himself bore our sins and live for righteousness; by his wounds you have been healed" (1 Peter 2:24). The verse is talking about sin and righteousness, not sickness and disease.

Therefore, being "healed "in both these verses is speaking of being forgiven and saved, not physically healed, but none of that matters if you don't have faith in Jesus neither one will work, the spiritual nor the physical.

Sometimes people are physically healed when they place their faith in Christ, but this is not always the case.

(1 John 5:14-15). God still performs miracles. God still heals people. Sickness, disease, pain, and death are still reality in this world.

(Revelation 21). We all need to be less preoccupied with our physical condition in this world and a lot more concerned with our spiritual condition.

(Revelation 21:4). Describes the true healing we should all be longing for: "He will wipe every tear from their eyes. There will be no more death or mourning or crying or pain, for the old order or things has passed away."

How is your energy level for our Heavenly Father?

Energy: The strength and vitality required for sustained physical or mental activity.

Measure of the ability of a body or system to do work or produce a change.

Now did you know that Satan wants to lead you around like a puppeteer?

He wants to have total control over your spirit in order to destroy you and your relationship with Jesus.

The Lord on the other hand wants to lead you as you should want to follow Him and that is of your own free will.

You have to remember God is not out to destroy you but to give you life after death.

Destroy means: To put an end to the existence of (something) by damaging or attacking it.

Let see: If I were to ask you a question dealing with the subject of change in your life would you be afraid to move ahead?

Sometimes we pray to God for answers, but at times it seems as though you're not being heard.

You being to get restless in your spirit because you see others around you being blessed.

Now the Bible says not to become **Jealous**: feeling resentment because of someone else's success or blessing.

Not to **Envy**: When you want what someone else has.

Did you know that there are 56 verses in the Bible that talk about jealousy and envy?

James 3: 16 Says For wherever there is jealousy and selfish ambition, there you will find disorder and envy/evil of every kind.

But when you are seeking God the right way your wanting him to put oppositions in your path in order to choose from so that you move up and ahead.

That's because in order to do what needs to be done in this day and age you need substance/finance/assets.

People are wanting to see what Jesus is actually doing for you.

Some people love to commit suicide it starts when you remove yourself from God's will, His way of living.

Because before you die in the flesh, you have to die in the spirit.

Did you know that you need to watch who you touch and who touches you?

Did you also know that people who commit suicide want to take from you that which they are afraid to receive from anymore for themselves; Jesus.

They don't want or like the new change so they become bord with the ways of God.

They begin to look at Jesus as a third-class God.

Because in their lives first comes me and then comes pleasing of the flesh and for some maybe after that comes Jesus.

Unlike the lady that had to press her way to Jesus.

Jesus has no need to press His way towards us, because He is the way the light and the truth.

Only through Him can you be saved and enter into the Heavenly Fathers Kingdom.

So, you better press towards Jesus every day when you wake up and before you go to bed as well as when you go through out your day A- men.

Did you also know that there are people who are out there saying if I could just touch his/ her spirit I can take them from Jesus?

In Mark 5:8 For she said, if I may touch but his clothes I shall be whole.

When someone takes our power we can't do or say what Jesus said in **Mark 5:30 At once Jesus realized that the power had gone out of Him, He turned around in the crowd and asked," who touched my clothes?**

God said that all spirits should be connected together through the blood of Jesus.

A lot of these people come after adults, teens and even children, which is sad because now days it's in the form of sex.

The people you sleep with that have demons living in their bodies can transfer what's in them into your body and once in your body it takes over your spirit.

That's when we go back to watch who you touch and who touches you.

Look for God's love the perfect relationship starts with Him.

Love is like the wind on a cool summer's night.

All is still except the movements and sounds of two hearts beating together as one.

Thump goes one thump goes the second.

They then begin to go thump, thump, thump in motion as one.

Just as the cycle of winter, spring, summer and fall all waiting patiently for their time to come not rushing or getting up-set with each other when one may take longer than the other, no matter how long one maybe.

I will always remember a word of advice from a friend of mine.

Never make yourself to seem new in an unfamiliar place and never look at anyone as a friend.

Because the devil is sure to pick you up and steal you away, unless you truly have Jesus in your life.

Even if that friend is your flesh.

One other reminder when you come into the church don't only bring in your body, but also bring in your spirit.

It is becoming seriously apparent that most people now live their lives in a way that is putting their spirits in jeopardy of losing the opportunity of the place that Jesus went to prepare for us.

Jesus said I go to prepare a place in my Father's house were 1000 years is like one day.

It seems as though they either don't believe in God or that there is a Heaven or Hell.

People are or they are becoming so money hunger that they are becoming non-responsive to other people because they only see themselves.

They are in a world that revolves around themselves and no one else matters.

They are failing to realize that they are hanging around with people like themselves and they are treating each other the same.

Take what you can get while they still have it.

Once you are no good to someone or have nothing to give you are tossed out with the trash.

A lot of times when people ask you questions about God or the Bible, it's not to find out how much you know about the Bible, but about your character.

Character: The mental and moral qualities distinctive to an individual.

How you live your life according to the Bible as how it says you should live.

Not judging or condemning someone without proof as well as if you are able to forgive as God and even Jesus forgave the world you and me.

Are you able to forgive yourself?

When I first began to write this book, I felt like I was a failure; I had gone through a failed marriage a business that it seemed everyone around me did nothing but put me down.

I need to say this; Jesus needed me to meet the people of my past in order for me to meet the new people of my future.

There will always come a time in our lives when we will find someone that we trust that will let us down but I need you to realize, God is not human so He will never let you down or break a promise.

Even though I was dealing with the last part of hurt and needing to come to a complete state of forgiveness in my spirit the release of what was needing to be was given to me through writing.

I was so afraid and ashamed to write about the anger I once had in my life that almost placed me in Hell.

Not saying that there couldn't still be that slight chance that I could end up there, but I am doing all I can not to go.

I had no idea of who I was and what I had did to the ones I loved.

Because I needed Jesus to show me Gods love and how I had to really believe in myself that He loved me.

Jesus had to show me where it started.

The problems in my life and how to start loving me again.

It's not easy and a lot of people are not realizing that in order to stop being mad at the world and everyone in it.

It starts with you, what I mean is when you stop hating your life and you begin to learn how to pray not get made or up-set with what someone else has or what they have accomplished in their lives that are different from yours.

As you do this praying on a daily basis in time things will still feel like God is not there in your life and others around you may seem to become blessed and having such great testimonies about all the good things going on in their lives.

If your heart has been broken how others seem to have out of nowhere had someone come into their lives and now they are a loving couple and they are now making plans to get married.

You begin to say to God what about me I would love to have someone in my life.

Silence.

Let his will be done.